SECRETS

OF

BUYING

PACKAGING MACHINERY

How to Win in a No-Win Game

Rich Frain and John R Henry

Illustrated by John R Henry and Troy Locker Palmer
Cover by Mike Jones and Troy Locker Palmer

Also by John R Henry

Machinery Matters: John Henry on Packaging, Machinery, Troubleshooting

Packaging Machinery Handbook

Achieving Lean Changeover: Putting SMED to Work

ISBN-13: 978-1502420176

ISBN-10: 1502420171

Dedication

This book is dedicated to all project managers, by whatever formal title, everywhere.

Some of us know what you go through on every project.

Special thanks go to Lisa Rampage Joerin for her invaluable patience and assistance in editing this book,

and to Debra Martino for the Bob & Joe illustrations.

CONTENTS

FORWARD

Based on my 38 years of experience in the packaging machinery industry, ninety percent of the projects I have worked on have not met the customer's expectations. At first I thought that it must be me, but over the years I have found that all venders feel the same.

Customers consistently call us when they are completely out of time. The samples they send us keep changing. The project objectives have not been agreed to by all stakeholders. The packaging required for set up and testing is always late. They decline expert start up and training. They think that complex machinery can simply be shipped, plugged in and production begins at full speed the next day.

Frain has sold over 25,000 machines to customers of all sizes and industries. We have developed a system called KEIS to help customers meet their delivery objectives. I have to say that it has met with only limited success. The purpose of this book and of our website is to help project managers and their teams to understand the steps needed to have a successful project. My personal objective is to get everyone a raise and a promotion.

I am fortunate to have had John Henry of Changeover.com as my partner in this endeavor. John has been a plant manager, business owner, writer, teacher and consultant for over 35 years in the packaging industries. John literally wrote the book on packaging machinery with his Packaging Machinery Handbook.

John developed and teaches IOPP Packaging Machinery Basics course, which Frain Industries has hosted for many years. I always enjoy sitting in on these classes as well as his seminars at PMMI conferences. He is able to make learning fun and all of his students leave with a solid knowledge of how packaging machinery functions.

-Rich Frain, 2013

CHAPTER 1

GETTING STARTED

In the beginning is the idea that initiates the buying process. It may come from marketing with an idea for a new package. It may come from engineering with an idea for a more efficient machine. It may come from the packaging floor with the idea of replacing an older or problematic machine. It may come from plant management with an idea for additional production capacity.

The idea will influence the buying process and priorities. If the machine is being bought for a new package, speed to market may be the most important driver in the decision. If being purchased to replace an existing, still-operable, machine, the time between purchase and delivery may not be as crucial. If the machine is being purchased to increase efficiency, that will be the driving force behind the project. Other situations will bring other priorities.

These motives may influence and vary the buying process, but, at the core, the process will always follow a similar path: Identify needs and parameters, develop a specification, select a vendor, purchase the machine and supervise its fabrication, install it and place it in production. Each step will be detailed in the following chapters.

THE IDEA BECOMES A PROCESS

Buying packaging machinery can be stressful. It is expensive. It takes a long time between initial concept and production—sometimes as much as eighteen to twenty-four months. The variety of choices can seem overwhelming. (There are over 100 companies making labeling machines just in the United States). The buyer, even the experienced buyer, may be purchasing machinery with which they have no familiarity at all. When buying from a non-domestic vendor there are often language, cultural, import/export, and currency issues as well.

JOE'S SECRET

During the process, there are often changes in direction and scope. Just when the project manager thinks they have all the questions answered, the package designers may decide to use a unique dispensing cap instead of the standard flat cap that had been contemplated. This may necessitate changes to the machine design or, depending on the machine, may necessitate a different machine from another vendor.

Once the machine has been specified and ordered, the project manager must stay on top of the project to assure that the vendor has all samples, payments, approvals, and anything else the vendor might need in a timely manner. The project manager must make sure that the vendor is on schedule and is building the machine that the buyer wanted and requested—not, due to miscommunication or other errors, something different.

Don't stress, and don't get pressured. Always take a methodical approach to the project.

When the machine is delivered and installed, management expects it to be like a new car, which starts up at the turn of the key. Packaging machinery almost never does. Once installed, there is a process of debugging and learning that delays production: sometimes by a little bit, sometimes by a lot. Management seldom understands this learning curve. They spent the money; they want to see some immediate return. They need to understand the concept of the learning curve. It can take three to six months for a plant to work its way up the learning curve from commissioning to full production.

Unlike many other purchases, there is only one chance to get it right. The time between purchase order and production is usually months. In some cases, it can be more than a year. If the purchase is not done correctly, it is not just a monetary loss. The time loss if the project has to be started again can dwarf the costs of purchase.

Packaging machines typically have a useful service life of 10–15 years. It can become considerably longer in some cases. Some labelers, originally designed and built in the 1930s are still in daily use today. Mistakes made in purchasing will be around for a long, long time.

Some larger companies have departments for buying packaging machinery. In many companies, purchases are made at the plant level. The packaging manager buying a new cartoner may buy machinery once every five years or so. He or she may never get a chance to gain significant experience in this process. Each machine purchase is a new experience and subject to new mistakes.

The word stressful may be too mild to describe the process.

In the end, the successful project makes it all worthwhile. There is a feeling of satisfaction seeing a smoothly running machine or a line making product for sale. That satisfaction can make the stress seem pretty minor after all is said and done.

The authors of this book have over 70 years of experience designing and building, buying and selling, installing and operating, maintaining and repairing virtually every type of packaging machine ever made as well as quite a bit of experience with process and other manufacturing equipment experience. The purpose of this book is to share that experience with the reader. The authors hope that sharing this experience takes as much mystery and stress as possible out of the process.

The book is organized into nine chapters. These chapters are designed to provide the reader with a step-by-step process for buying packaging machinery. This includes determining what the user will need; why there is never enough time; how much it is worth and how to pay for it; environmental considerations related to where and how the machine will be used; machine-specific considerations; development of the specifications; machine fabrication; and testing, commissioning, and supporting the machine after installation.

Buying packaging machinery entails risks at all stages in the process. By following the process in this book, buyers will not eliminate these risks, but they will reduce them.

USED OR PRE-OWNED MACHINERY

JOE'S SECRET

When thinking of packaging machinery, many people focus on new machines. In many cases, used machinery may be the better option—not just because of price.

What is "used"?

Used machinery is machinery that has been previously sold. In many, though not all, cases, it was used in production. Used machinery can be purchased at auction (either in-person or online), on E-Bay, business to business, through used machinery brokers and dealers, and occasionally from the original machine builder. Used machinery is not always "used." In some cases, the machinery may be brand-new—still in the factory shipping crate—or it may have

"Used" machinery is sometimes brand-new.

been installed but has never run. There is also a special case of intra-company used machinery. This is machinery that was at one time purchased new by a company, either used in production or not, and then made available to another plant or line within the same company. In general, it is similar to machinery purchased outside of the company except that its provenance may be better known and pricing, if any, will be determined by internal company practices.

When applied to packaging machinery, the term used is a complex term and covers a range of situations. At one end of the scale is the machine sold "as is, where is" by the current user to another user. In this type of sale, it is strictly caveat emptor or let the buyer beware. The buyer is normally responsible for removing the machine from its existing location and moving the machine to the destination plant as well as doing any repairs, refurbishing, upgrading, or modification that might be required. The buyer may get an attractive price in this transaction, but he or she also takes the risks that the total cost of the machine—required work to put it in running order, modifications as needed for the buyer's product, and installation in the buyer's plant—may exceed any monies saved in the initial purchase price.

Another way to purchase used machinery is through a broker. Brokers can range from one person with a cell phone and laptop working from a kitchen table to large, multinational operations. Brokers are the traditional and much-maligned middleman, but they perform useful functions. The broker knows who is selling the machinery and who is looking for that type of machinery, and the broker brings them together. In a specialized market such as machinery, this matching of buyer and seller is a valuable service. Brokers may also have product expertise that the buyer may lack. Brokers are generally paid by commission by the seller—with their commission being a percentage of the sales price. Brokers may sometimes be paid by the seller or may receive commissions from both. The smart buyer will remember that the broker is representing, in theory at least, whoever is paying them.

Stocking used machinery dealers differ from brokers in that they take ownership of the machinery and then hold it in inventory until they can find a buyer. Some of these are little more than warehouses for used machinery.

At the top end of the scale is the Quality Pre-owned Machinery Dealer. The Quality Pre-owned Machinery Dealer takes almost all of the risk and work of buying a packaging machine from the buyer's hands. It makes the experience of purchasing a pre-owned machine comparable (but faster and less expensive) to purchasing a new machine.

Services offered by a Quality Pre-owned Machinery Dealer include:

- Large onsite inventory to select from.
- Rigorous inspection of all machines prior to placing in inventory
- Engineering services to assure proper selection.
- Design engineering services for required modifications to run a customer's product.
- Control engineers and technicians to upgrade PLC and other electronic control systems as well as integrate multiple machines.
- Complete shop facilities for refurbishment and modification.
- Facilities for factory acceptance testing (FAT).

- Quality assurance program for all machines sold.

- Original manuals for all machines in paper and electronic formats.

- Extensive spare parts inventory.

- Field service technicians for installation, commissioning and ongoing service.

- In-house rental, financing and leasing options.

There are a few companies which remanufacture packaging machinery for resale. Generally they specialize in a specific make or type of machine. These companies purchase used machines—such as rotary cappers—and replace all shafts, bearings, electronics, and any other worn or obsolete parts. They may add upgrades such as modern safety guarding, PLCs (Programmable Logic Controllers), and servo motors. They are essentially building a new machine using the basic components of the old machine as a starting point.

JOE'S SECRET

Never ignore the potential benefits of "used" machinery for any project

Pros and Cons of Used Machinery

Some people are hesitant to consider used machinery for their project, and there are a number of pros and cons. On the pro side, there are the following points:

- Price: The first benefit that comes to most minds when buying used machinery is price. The price of used machinery will almost always be significantly less expensive than a comparable new machine. One needs to be careful when buying solely on price since it is cost, not price, that is the critical parameter. Price is a one-time expense. Cost is paid every day after the machine has been purchased. Costs can include the cost of removal of the machine from its current location, transport, refurbishment, any modifications to meet the project needs, installation and debugging and—once in production—ongoing operating costs. A machine purchased "as is, where is" may look like a bargain until all of the after-purchase costs add up. Machinery costs - new and used - are discussed in depth in chapter 3 of this book.

- Availability: Other than a few standard, off-the-shelf items like coders, most packaging machinery is built to order rather than to stock. Delivery times are typically measured in months, and some large machines may take up to 9 months to a year or longer for delivery after the order has been placed. Used machines have already been built and can usually be modified for the new product in a few weeks or less. Some cartoners, fillers, cappers, and other machines are universal enough that there may be no modifications necessary, and the machine can ship in days rather than weeks.

- Proven designs: The last thing any manufacturer needs, especially one trying to introduce a new product, is to have their machine design be new and untested. A used machine has proven itself in service, and both its good and bad points are known. Some companies still build machines that are basically the same as machines they built in the 1950s because these machines have proven themselves over time. Machine builders are constantly upgrading their designs to include new features and new designs that they hope will work better. In many cases they do, but even Babe Ruth did not hit home runs all the time. Sometimes it just makes sense to stick with a proven design.

- Construction: Many older machines were built of cast iron and forgings. This gives them a rigidity and stability that many users favor. This is not always found in newer machines.

- Regulatory compliance: A company may have a regulatory requirement for a specific make and model that is no longer available.

- Standardization: In a similar vein, some companies wish to standardize their packaging lines even when there may not be any regulatory requirement to do so. When the standard machines are no longer available, used machinery may be the only way to accomplish this.

- Simplicity: Modern machines are chock-full of servos, PLCs, and other modern electronic components. Developments in this area have greatly enhanced machine efficiency, reliability, and ease of operation and maintenance. However, not all plants have the technical staff to work with this technology. Difficulties in maintenance may overwhelm any benefits from greater simplicity. If a company is not willing to make the training or staffing investments, older mechanical and electrical machinery may be the better choice. In some areas of the world, and even some parts of the United States, it may not be possible to hire a suitable workforce even if the company is willing to make the investment.

- Specialization: Over the years, brilliant people have developed highly specialized machines for niche packages. The options for those with similar products may be either a new custom machine or a used machine originally designed for that product.

- "Try before you buy": The used machine already exists, and it may be possible to see it in operation either with your product or a similar product.

- Rental: Some Quality Pre-owned Machinery Dealers have rental programs. This allows the machine to be placed in production and run for an extended period to confirm that it is the right machine for the job.

- Sole source: Many packaging machinery projects involve multiple machines joined together to form a packaging line. When buying new, this may require dealing with several different vendors and coordinating all machines to work with each other. There will be several factory acceptance tests (FATs) in different locations. A large stocking dealer of used machinery will often be able to supply all the machines to make up the complete line. The dealer can assemble the machines in their shops then make and debug all utility and mechanical interconnections. This allows the buyer to perform a FAT on a complete, integrated line rather than piecemeal. Any glitches in interconnections and controls can be resolved in the vendor's shop before shipment. When the line arrives at the buyer's plant, it is ready to be installed and commissioned by remaking the previous connections.

On the other hand, there are some potential drawbacks to buying used rather than new machinery:

- Known or potential contamination: When buying used machinery, one must know its provenance. If a machine was previously used on a product that was incompatible with the product to be run, trace contamination could cause a problem. In today's litigious society, even the possibility of contamination can lead to serious problems.

- Cost of refurbishing and/or modifying: There are some exceptions, but generally, any used machine will require refurbishing, which may mean anything from simple cleaning to replacement of worn components. In many cases, the machine will require modification—if only fitting of change parts—to make the machine ready for the new product. These add to the acquisition cost of the machine. In some cases, they can add enough to eat up any potential savings.

- Hidden defects: No matter how carefully the used machine is investigated and inspected before buying and how much good faith there is between buyer and seller, it is still possible for a machine to have defects that were not found at the time of sale. Assuming that these defects can be corrected, they will add to the cost of the machine.

Many of the cons listed occur less because the machinery is used than because of who the machine is purchased from. A Quality Pre-Owned Machinery Dealer , with a deep inventory of machines to choose from—and with well-qualified engineering, fabrication, service and support staffs—renders most of the objections moot. Some will have extensive libraries of manuals as well as extensive inventories of spare parts.

These libraries allow them to provide original factory manuals. The spare parts inventory allows them to support machines that the original build either will not or cannot support.

DEFINITIONS

This book will try to use language common to the packaging industry. Some of these terms can be ambiguous. Original equipment manufacturer (OEM) is one example. Some use the term to refer to the original builder of the packaging machine. It can also mean the manufacturer of standard purchased components such as motors. To avoid confusion, this book uses the following definitions:

JOE'S SECRET

Make sure everyone is using the same terms to avoid miscommunications.

Batch/Lot

The terms batch and lot are often used interchangeably. Both mean a discrete quantity of product. The actual quantity may be determined by physical limitations such as mixing tank or oven size or by formulation constraints. Batch size can be expressed in input quantity (for example, 2,000 gallons of shampoo or 8,000 pounds of potato chips). Alternately, it may be characterized by output such as 20,000 bottles of shampoo or 40,000 bags of potato chips. In many processes, each package will carry a code identifying which batch it was produced from. This book will use the term batch and batch size rather than lot and lot size.

In some continuous processes such as beverage canning, the batch will be based on a time interval (for example, all beer canned during a day from midnight to midnight).

Buyer

As used in this book, the buyer will be the company purchasing the machine for production use. Another common term is end user. A company may have a number of people and functions involved in the machine purchase. These include marketing, engineering, finance, purchasing, and packaging to name a few. The term buyer will be used generically to include all the people involved in purchasing the machine. Where a distinction must be made about the individual responsible for technical aspects of the purchase, they will be referred to as the project manager.

Changeover

The term changeover, as used in this book, means the total process that takes place to convert a packaging machine or line from running one product to another. It is not to be confused with setup, which is defined below.

Changeover Time

Changeover time is the total elapsed time from when one production batch ends until the next production batch is running at normal speed and efficiency.

Changeparts

Changeparts are product and/or package specific parts that are used to convert a machine from one product to another.

Component

Components are assembled to make a package. The term component will be used in its broad sense in this book. Components will include discrete components like bottles and caps or continuous materials, such as the film used in forming pouches and bags. Packaging components, as the term is used in this book will also include supplies such as glue or tape that may not always be thought of as components per se.

Factory Acceptance Test (FAT)
Upon completion of the machine but prior to shipment a factory acceptance test is always in order. This test will be described in detail in Chapter 7. In brief, it is a test during which the machine is run with the buyer present. It should simulate, as far as possible actual production conditions and is intended to demonstrate that the machine meets all specifications and design requirements.

Original Equipment Manufacturer (OEM)
Original equipment manufacturer (OEM) and can have two distinct meanings. In some cases, it may be used to denote the company that originally built the packaging machine. In other cases, it is used to denote companies that supply component parts to the machine builder such as motors, PLCs, air cylinders, sensors and the like. To avoid confusion, this book will use OEM in the latter sense of standard components. The builder of the machine will be referred to as the vendor or machine builder, not the OEM

Operator
The term operator will be used generically in this book to refer to teammates on the plant floor charged with routine operation of the machinery. In the case of semi-automated and manual packaging operations, they will be doing actual packaging. In the case of automated machinery, their focus will tend to be more on replenishing supply hoppers, monitoring the machine for proper operation, correcting minor jams, and cleaning before and after the batch. In some plants, they may perform some or all of the machinery changeover.

Package
The package is the assemblage of components and products that make up the final package as sold to the end consumer.

Product
The product is the candy in the carton, the chicken in the bag, or the bottles in the box. It is the end product that the customer is buying.

Purchase
Most packaging machinery is sold via straight sale. Some is not sold but is either leased or rented. For the most part, the commercial part of the transaction does not affect the concepts in this book and the terms purchase or buy will be used generically to mean acquisition by whatever means.

Setup

The term setup is sometimes used interchangeably with the term changeover, but they are not the same thing. There are many other activities that need to take place during a changeover including machine and room cleaning, material movement, documentation, startup (the period between when the line starts and when it settles down to run normally) just to name a few. Setup refers to the specific tasks of modifying the machine, either by changing package specific parts or by adjustment. Setup is an important part of changeover, but it is still only a part.

Technician

There may be various crafts charged with diagnosis, repair, maintenance, adjustment, setup, installation, and other technical tasks. In most plants, these will be packaging mechanics—though they can also be millwrights, electricians, programmers, or others. This book will use the term technician inclusively to refer to all of them.

Vendor

Packaging machinery is sold through a number of different channels. It is most often sold directly by the machine builder. In some cases, it will be sold through distributors, agencies or brokers. In order to avoid confusion, the term vendor in this book will be used to mean the company that originally built the machine regardless of which sales channel it may flow through. It will also include stocking used machinery dealers when they provide substantial services such as upgrades, factory acceptance testing and other services normally provided by machinery manufacturers.

JOE'S SECRET

The biggest secret to my success?

Involve everyone in the project,
from the floor mechanic and operator,
all the way up the line.

CHAPTER 2

THE RACE

It's a race against time, and it's already too late.

What the project manager really needs is a time machine to provide some breathing room.

Modern companies move faster and faster with fewer and fewer resources. Twenty years ago a project might have had a dedicated project manager and allow 12 to 18 months for completion. Today, management expects it to be done by the maintenance manager or regular engineering staff and completed in 6 months—all while performing their regular duties. This sounds like an impossible challenge, and it is, which is why it can be the no-win game of this book's title.

The race starts the moment someone gets an itch for a new packaging machine. The reasons for the machine will vary.

Contract packagers reduce risk and increase flexibility for brand owners. Contract packagers are independent, third-party firms that manufacture and package the brand owner's products. When a new product is launched, initial production volumes are higher than normal in order to fill the store shelves. When product sales exceed forecasts, the contract packager picks up the slack. What contract packagers have to offer the brand owner is, first and foremost, flexibility. In addition to flexibility, contract packagers absorb some of the risk of inaccurate forecasts, product success, and product failure. When contract packagers need a new machine, it is often to fulfill a contract they are bidding on. Winning a new contract can be a good-news/bad-news situation. The good news is that they got the contract. The bad news is that they got the contract. If they are late getting into production, they may lose the contract. More importantly, they will lose their reputation. They may even be sued for damages into the bargain.

JOE'S SECRET

Buyers are responsible for more project delays than vendors.

They can't afford to lose this race.

A drug company may have a new, patented drug coming to market. While it is on patent, it might sell for $1.50 per tablet. When the patent expires, generic competitors might force the price to $0.50 per tablet. Each day of delay in getting into production during the patent window represents one less day of patent protection. More to the point—it represents one less day of $1.50 sales.

They can't afford to lose this race.

A vegetable processor may need the machine installed in time for the August harvest. If they do not have the machine up and running in July, they will have spent the money for nothing. The machine will sit idle until the following August.

They can't afford to lose this race.

A toothpaste manufacturer may be ready to launch a unique product. Each day of delay in the project is another day a competitor may hear of it and beat them to the starting line. The innovator winds up playing catch-up to the copier, and that seldom ends well.

They can't afford to lose this race.

Sometimes the machine is simply needed to replace an existing machine that has seen better days. Too much delay could leave the plant with no machine if the replacement has been put off too long.

They can't afford to lose this race.

And so it goes.

There are a lot of opportunities to get a machine project wrong and only a few to get it right. Getting it right is important to a company's tactical success as excess costs come out of profit. More importantly, getting it right can be critical to the strategic success of a company. There is one "800-pound gorilla" that accounts for 40% to 70% of sales at most consumer packaged goods (CPG) manufacturers: This single customer won't do much to a company that fails to give them what they want, when, and where they want it. They just won't buy from them. Few companies can withstand the loss of a customer of this size. The project has to be right. Getting projects consistently right is one of the things that make a company an industry leader.

Every project is a race against time. It is a race that is easy to lose and harder to win. The project manager must stay on top of the project at all times to make sure that delays do not creep in. The project manager has direct control over some of these delays and will be able to influence some of the others.—Some the project manager will be able to do nothing about. The wise project manager will recognize which are which. The wise project manager will also realize that no matter whose fault it is, it will be the project manager who will get the blame. Management will not care that the project was delayed because the finance department did not get the down payment check out in time. They will not care that the converter failed to ship samples to the vendor. Management will not care that their expectations were unrealistic. All management will care about is that the project manager was late with production, and it is costing the company money.

JOE'S SECRET

NOTHING happens until the vendor gets their downpayment check!

Delays are impossible to eliminate, but the savvy project manager can do a lot to minimize them. One way is to go with an experienced and reliable vendor rather than try to save every last nickel possible on the purchase price. Chapter 3 will discuss in detail the need to focus on cost—including the costs of being late—rather than on price. The experienced and reliable vendor will know what is possible and what is not. This vendor provides trustworthy, realistic schedules and will meet them—if the project manager does his or her part getting everything in on time.

Then, when the project comes in ahead of schedule and under budget, the project manager is the hero instead of the goat. If the project manager is lucky, management will recognize this. If not, at least the project manager has the quiet self-satisfaction of a job well done.

Frain Industries, a large Quality Pre-owned Machinery Dealer , analyzed 10,000 projects for which they had provided used machinery. They found that the total project time from initial definition to startup was 22–35 weeks. If the 4–6 weeks of learning curve to fully efficient production is considered, it was 26–41 weeks.

This was for machines that were already built, and actual preparation time (customizing the machine to buyer specifications) was only 11 weeks (using middle values) or one third of the total project time to fully efficient production. If a new machine is being purchased, this preparation/building time will be longer. Even so, if the vendor's build time is 20 weeks instead of 11 weeks, it will be still be less than half the total project time.

Some vendors being considered may be able to offer faster delivery than others. If delivery time is critical, this will weigh in their favor; however, once selected, there is not much that can be done to speed preparation/building time. Sometimes the buyer may be able to shave a few days by paying premium overtime. On an 11-week build, this might allow delivery 1 week sooner. On a 20-week build, it might allow 2 weeks to be shaved off delivery. It will rarely be more and will often be less.

So if the builder/dealer can't do much to deliver more quickly, it's hopeless. Right?

Actually, no. There are a number of things the buyer can do to improve delivery. Frain Industries analyzed over 10,000 projects. This chart shows the breakdown of project time. Other than machine build and—perhaps to some extent—shipping, all of these delays are controlled by the buyer, not the vendor.

For example, sending samples (1.5 weeks), making a decision (1.5 weeks) and sending the down payment check (2.5 weeks) took a total of 5.5 weeks or about 20% of the time between commencing the project and putting the machine in production. It is important for the project manager to forcefully explain the importance of getting the down payment check out. The vendor will do nothing, nothing at all, until the check is received. It is the job of the finance department to hold on to the company's money as long as possible, but in this case, it is counterproductive. The few dollars the company saves by slow payment will be offset many times over by the cost of project delays. A 3-week delay in getting the check out might result in a 6-week delay in project completion. The finance department must understand not only how much of a delay they are causing but the cost, in dollars, of that delay.

The learning curve—from commissioning to fully efficient production—took 5 weeks. While there will always be a learning curve, it can be shortened with better training and more attention to detail.

Better project management will dramatically reduce the total project time. Poorer project management can increase the time significantly.

Many project managers as well as others involved in the buying process do not understand how machines are built. Most packaging machines—especially

TIMELINE
(TIME IN WEEKS)

PROJECT DEFINITION(1-2)
VENDOR RESEARCH(1-2)
VENDOR PROPOSALS(1-2)
VENDOR SELECTION(1-2)
DOWNPAYMENT(1-2)
SAMPLES TO VENDOR(1-2)
SIGNED WORKSCOPE(1-2)
MACHINE BUILD(10-12)
FAT AT VENDOR(1-2)
CRATING & SHIPPING
UNCRATING, SETTING & CONNECTING(1-2)
STARTUP & TRAINING(1-2)
LEARNING CURVE TO FULLY EFFICIENT PRODUCTION (4-6)

PROJECT DURATION
26 TO 41 WEEKS
Data courtesy Frain Industries

larger ones—are built one at a time starting when the builder receives the purchase order, samples, and down payment. Depending on workload, the build may not even start immediately. The builder often needs to finish a current project to free up floor space, technicians, and other resources before they can start on the next one. Even if the resources are immediately available, there will be delays as the builder needs to order and receive raw materials and OEM components.

Many builders try to maintain some order backlog to avoid having unused resources waiting for the next project. This helps keep costs (and prices!) down, but it does put pressure on the buyer to assure that everything is provided to the builder when required.

Buyers sometimes seem to be under the impression that a 1-week delay in providing requested materials will not delay the project at all. More frequently, they seem to believe that being a week late providing samples will result in only a 1-week delay in project completion. What they fail to realize is that the vendor is likely to be working on multiple projects at the same time. If the vendor cannot continue working on the buyer's project because of delays in buyer response, they will move the company's resources to another job. This means that the buyer has fallen in priority in the vendor's production queue. The buyer's 1-week delay in providing an approval or samples may result in 2, 3, or more weeks delay in completion of their machine.

Nowhere is this more important than in the initial stages of the project. When the vendor makes their proposal to the buyer, they will specify an estimated delivery time. This is often worded along the lines of "Estimated delivery is 10–12 weeks after receipt of order, down payment, and samples. This estimate is based on current shop load." Too many buyers tend to look at this and only see the 10 weeks, seldom the 12 weeks. Worse, it sometimes seems like they think the 10 weeks began counting with the initial phone call to the vendor.

It is the project manager's responsibility to make sure that all materials and approvals are submitted on time. The vendor probably won't take the initiative in pushing for them. The vendor may benefit from samples being late since it alleviates some of the pressure for finishing the machine by the promised date. Delivery will be delayed by 4 weeks? It's the buyer's fault for being a week late with the samples. Sometimes that is true; sometimes it is not. It doesn't matter. The project is still 4 weeks late, and company management will blame the project manager.

JOE'S SECRET

Make sure there is a single point of contact for all technical issues.

ASSIGN A PROJECT MANAGER

Whenever a machine is built to order rather than built for inventory, scheduling is critical. Vendors can find scheduling hard enough to do accurately under the best of conditions; buyers can sometimes make it more difficult than it needs to be.

Both vendor and buyer should assign a project manager to handle all technical communications between them. All communication must be funneled through these two project managers. These single points of contact help keep communication on track as well as help avoid miscommunication. In some cases, there will be a separate contact for commercial questions such as credit checks, payments, and the like. Even though this may not be the responsibility of the project manager, the project manager must take care to stay fully informed.

Vendors require the buyer to provide certain things without which they cannot proceed. Machine delivery schedules are predicated on the vendor receiving these in a timely manner. When schedules are not timely provided, serious and escalating project delays will result.

Down Payment

Most vendors, when accepting an order, will require a down payment. Most vendors will not lock a job into the production schedule until they receive the down payment. It will generally be the responsibility of the buyer's purchasing department to take care of this, but the project manager must still verify that the payment has been sent. The project manager must close the loop by making sure the vendor has received the payment and it has not been lost in the mail. This may seem redundant as it should normally be the responsibility of the commercial contact. Nevertheless, if there are any delays caused by this, it is the project manager's head on the chopping block.

Samples

Samples are another key issue that the project manager needs to stay on top of.

Vendors will need samples for two different purposes: engineering and testing. The samples sent for making the initial proposal must never be relied on. If the vendor has not discarded the samples, they may have been damaged, or the buyer may have modified them. In order to avoid problems, it is imperative that fresh samples be sent to the vendor to allow them to do final engineering. Samples should be exactly like those to be run. If stoppers are to be lubricated prior to insertion, lubricated stoppers must be sent. If there will be mold flash on the bottles, representative bottles with flash must be sent. If there are two suppliers for the same cap, send samples from both. Any special conditions like these must also be called out to the vendor to assure that they take them into account.

JOE'S SECRET

Buyer failure to get samples to the vendor on time will prevent the vendor from delivering the machine on time.

The vendor will generally need these engineering samples immediately upon acceptance of the purchase order. They will probably advise what quantities are required but if not, the project manager must ask. Never assume and never skimp on samples. Better for vendor to have too many samples than to not have enough.

Representative testing samples must also be supplied to the vendor in quantity in addition to engineering samples. These will be used for testing of machine functions during the build as well as for final testing of the completed machine. Some vendors may require final testing samples at the time of order. In other cases, especially if bulky, vendors may specify a different date for which samples are needed. Some products, such as frozen foods, may need to be supplied at specific time so that testing can occur while frozen. Still other products may change with age. One shampoo-like product in the author's experience changed its liquid properties dramatically when not used for the 1–2 weeks between buyer shipment and vendor receipt. In that case, special arrangements were made to express ship samples to arrive on the days that test runs were planned.

As with the engineering samples, the project manager must make sure that these are sent in a timely manner. The project manager must also assure that they are received by the vendor. Tracking the shipment via the carrier is fine, but there is no substitute for speaking directly with the vendor to make sure that the samples were received and are in good condition.

The project manager must provide the vendor with material safety data sheets (MSDS) where appropriate. Unless the product is easily cleanable with standard detergents or solvents, they must also explain how to clean it after testing as well as how to dispose of it. Vendors may simply pack up all the samples and return them to the buyer with the machine. If other means of disposal are to be used, this must be negotiated between buyer and vendor.

Approvals

Typically the vendor's engineering department will produce drawings of the machine, showing how it is to be built to meet the buyer's specifications. These are the drawings— usually referred to as "shop drawings"—that will be used to fabricate the machine. The buyer must carefully inspect these drawings to assure that what is being proposed is what was requested. In addition to the project manager, the packaging manager, packaging supervisor, maintenance manager, maintenance mechanic, operators and everyone else who will be running or maintaining the machine after installation must sign off as well.

Failure to have everyone sign will result in finger pointing, and all involved saying that they would never have let this or that issue happen if they had known. Everyone's approval is required upfront. This makes it their machine and gives them an ownership interest in making sure that it works.

Multiple reviews make it more likely that an issue that one person missed will be caught by another. One project manager did not take sufficient care to do this and—on a visit to the vendor—found that they had begun fabricating a left-handed machine when a right-handed machine had been specified. The vendor had made an error on the shop drawings, but the project manager did not catch it when it was approved. This stage is the time and the place to catch any errors. Delivery delays may be the least of the problems if the drawings are not carefully reviewed and approved. Correcting errors on paper is always easier than correcting them once fabrication has begun.

As with down payments and samples as discussed above, these drawings need to be approved and returned to the vendor as soon as possible. It is the project manager's life to be something of a pest. The project manager must keep bugging everyone until all the required approvals are in. Failure to timely return the approvals will create delivery delays.

Milestones must be an important part of any project schedule. Typical milestones can include: shop drawing approval, frame construction complete, electrical wiring complete, and so on. Some milestones may trigger a progress payment due from the buyer. As with the down payment, the project manager must to make sure that this is issued and received by the vendor in a timely manner. Some vendors have been known to stop working when a progress payment is past due.

SCHEDULING

It is easy to get lost in strange territory without a road map. Machinery buying is uncharted territory for many, and even the experienced project manager can find it easy to get lost. A road map is essential. In a packaging machine project, the road map is the master schedule. Every project must have a schedule, and the schedule must exist on paper or on a computer and must be shared. A schedule in the project manager's mind is not good enough.

The machine is only one part of the schedule. The schedule must include everything involved with the project. Some of the other things that need to be in the schedule may include hiring and training additional operators and technicians, remodeling or construction of the packaging room, installation or upgrade of utilities, developing SOPs and other documentation, and more. Some of these, like room renovation, may not be the project manager's direct responsibility. On the other hand, they do impact the overall length of the project. When the project gets delayed because the room is not ready, the project manager's boss is unlikely to accept "It's not my job/fault" as an excuse. When the project is late, the project manager gets the blame.

There are a couple of widely used project scheduling techniques that can be very helpful:

Gantt or Bar Charts

A Gantt chart is a type of bar chart that shows the schedule graphically. They have the advantage of being relatively easy to develop and maintain as well as being relatively easy to interpret, even for a person seeing one for the first time.

The project is divided into major tasks or milestones and listed in chronological order on the left side of the chart. A horizontal bar—scaled to the time duration of the task—is placed beside it. The bar is offset to the right to correspond with when it starts and ends. End date will be the right end of the bar. The bar may be shaded, or a second bar can be added underneath each task bar to show progress to date. This can be further refined by using red for tasks behind schedule, blue for tasks that are ahead, and green for tasks on schedule or some other color code.

This chart gives an excellent visual indication of exactly where the project is at any given moment. More importantly, it directs attention to delays.

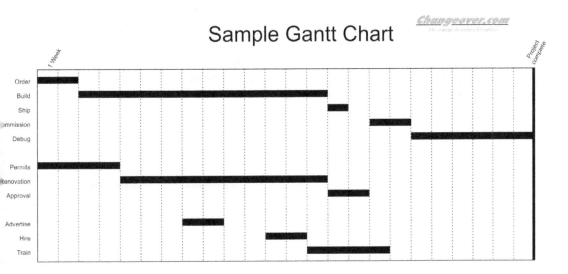

PERT/CPM

One of the drawbacks of Gantt charts is that they are sometimes not clear in displaying precedence or dependencies. In building a machine, construction of the frame must precede the start of electrical wiring. Network scheduling provides a graphic relation between all tasks clearly showing the precedence (what tasks have to happen before the next one can be started).

The two common network scheduling techniques are: PERT (Program Evaluation and Review Technique) and CPM (critical path method). They were originally developed for different purposes (Polaris submarines and chemical plants) and have some important differences though both appear similar. In current practice, both have come to generically be called PERT charts, and that term will be used here.

PERT charts identify all tasks in a project and completion times for each—just as in a Gantt chart. Unlike most Gantt charts, they more clearly identify which tasks must be done in sequence and which tasks can be done in parallel.

Most projects have multiple, parallel sets of tasks. A hypothetical machinery project might have three:

- Machinery purchase including building and testing
- Renovation of the packaging room
- Hiring and training additional employees for the new machine

The "critical path" in a network schedule is the longest combination of task completion times. In the case shown below, this is the renovation path indicated in bold. There are a number of programs that allow Gantt and PERT charts to be plotted and maintained on a PC or a tablet. These are very helpful, but the smart project manager will not rely on "pulling" the schedule from a computer. The smart project manager will print out the schedule and post it on the wall in front of his or her desk so that it "pushed" at them. As the schedule is updated, at least weekly, the project manager prints and reposts it so the current version is always displayed.

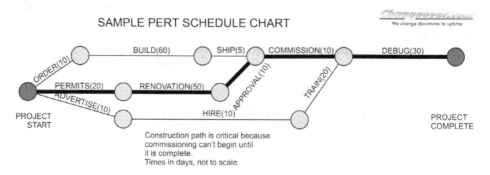

SAMPLE PERT SCHEDULE CHART

Construction path is critical because commissioning can't begin until it is complete.
Times in days, not to scale.

Printed copies of the initial and updated schedules must be circulated to everyone involved in the project. When a task is behind schedule, this must be called out, preferably in red. This is in addition to direct follow-up with the responsible person by the project manager, of course. Some recipients will prefer electronic copies and should receive them, but paper copies must be circulated as well. It is too easy to miss or ignore a schedule attached to an e-mail. It is more difficult—though not impossible—to ignore a paper copy.

Forward and Backward Scheduling

There are two ways to develop a schedule: forward and backward. Forward scheduling has a known start date. Each task is listed with its completion time and—based on the total task times—the completion date is calculated. If the project starts on January 1 and has a four-month estimated completion time, the project should complete on May 1.

Backward scheduling begins with a target completion or due date. In the example of the vegetable processor given earlier in the chapter, the due date is August 1, prior to the August harvest. As before, tasks and times are listed, and a project start date is calculated. If the processor needs the machine in operation for August 1 and completion time is estimated at four months, they must start the project no later than April 1.

Starting on April 1 would be foolish for a hard August 1 deadline. Times are always estimates and seldom fixed—no matter how well estimated. In order to meet the August deadline, the machine should be ordered no later than February 1 or so. They might tell the vendor, when ordering, that they do not need the machine shipped until July 1 (to allow time for installation and commissioning), but they should still get the order, samples, down payment, and anything else in as soon as possible. This reduces everyone's stress level, which is always a good thing.

JOE'S SECRET

Some vendors will want to ship the machine as soon as it is ready. The plant that needs the machine delivered for July installation may still be constructing or renovating the facility in June. If the machine shows up then, there may be no place to store it. If this is an issue, the vendor must be aware that—even though the order is being placed earlier than necessary for a July first delivery—the buyer will not accept earlier delivery.

More project delays are caused by the buyer than the vendor. Be sure you get the vendor what they need, when, or before, they need it.

Conversely, if a buyer has specified a July 1 delivery but does not have the facility ready in time, they must notify the vendor as soon as possible. If the vendor cannot ship the machine on schedule, the vendor may have a problem with this machine taking up shop space that is required for other projects. The vendor may also want to be paid for the machine even though—through no fault of their own—they have not shipped it. The buyer must be aware of these issues and make mutually acceptable arrangements.

Time.

There is never enough.

Only proper management of time allows the buyer to win the race.

CHAPTER 3

PRICE OR COST?

*"An engineer is someone who can do for 10 shillings
what anyone else can do for a pound [20 shillings]"* —Nevil Shute

Most packaging machinery represents a major investment. Even small, simple packaging machines can cost $25,000 and more. Larger, more complex machines can cost several million dollars. The project manager must understand the financial as well as the engineering elements of the project.

PRICE VERSUS COST

The first thing to understand about the process is that while the purchase price is always a relevant factor in a machine purchase, it is seldom the most important factor. If price becomes the focus, the project will be less successful that it might have otherwise been. The only relevant factor is cost—of which price is only a part.

Sometimes it is hard for a company to keep this in mind. Price is highly visible. It appears on the proposals; it appears on the purchase order, and it is remembered when the checks are issued. Some additional costs will be out of pocket such as the transport of the machine from the seller to the plant. Other costs are diffused and not as visible. These include the cost of the maintenance department's time to install the machine, the higher cost of repair parts because the machine was not built using standard components, increased downtime and other inefficiencies, reduced quality due to an inability to hold tight tolerances, and more.

The pain of these costs will be ongoing long after the joy of a low purchase price is forgotten.

The job of the purchasing manager is to make sure that acquisition costs, which are often interpreted as the purchase price, are kept as low as possible. The job of the project manager must be to make sure that total costs, including purchase price, are kept as low as possible. This may require the project manager to justify a higher-priced machine as the optimal selection. To do this, they need a thorough understanding of costs in general and the project's cost in particular.

The first place that this distinction can be blurred is in the initial proposal from the vendor. There is an old joke about the fellow who goes to buy a car:

> "Only $5,000." says the salesman.
>
> "I'll take it."
>
> "You will need to buy wheels and a motor too. That's an additional $15,000" the salesman then tells him.

Few vendors are this blatant but most proposals will have a base machine price and then a variety of options. Some of these may be necessary to a particular project. Others may be simply nice to have. Still others will not be applicable. Occasionally vendors will omit some important optional feature because they do not understand the requirements or because they made a good faith error. This can lead to surprises, delays, and bad feelings later on. It is important to be sure that the price on the proposal includes the costs of everything required to perform the necessary functions.

JOE'S SECRET

Be sure you understand what you are buying.

In fairness to the vendor, there will be legitimate instances where a price change after the machine has been ordered is justified. This may be due to a change in customer requirements, differences between quoting and testing samples, or a simple error. Most buyers and vendors will be dealing with each other in good faith. When this is so, these differences can usually be resolved amicably by negotiation.

In addition to machine options, there will be other items that should be included in the vendor's proposal. These can include crating, initial spare parts inventory, special documentation for customs, factory acceptance testing (FAT) and commissioning, and training.

LIFE CYCLE COST

The cost of the machine does not stop with the purchase. The relevant cost in machine selection is the total life cycle cost or the total cost of owning the machine over its life— from acquisition to disposal. As the saying goes "Forecasting is hard, especially about the future." True as that may be, the buyer must still make the best attempt possible to identify and quantify all the costs that the machine will incur.

JOE'S SECRET

It's COST, not PRICE that is the key to success

Virtually all packaging machines have what are called "wear parts." These are parts that will wear in normal use and must be replaced on a normal basis. Wear parts include things like suction cups, drive belts, and "O" rings. The number of wear parts as well as replacement frequency must be considered. In many cases, more important than the cost of the parts themselves is how hard the parts are to replace. The harder they are to replace, the greater the downtime and the more mechanic's time that will be needed. The harder they are to replace, the more likely it is that the machine will be run with worn parts leading to efficiency losses.

Suction cups are one example of a part that is not replaced as frequently as they should be. They are inexpensive, and in some operations may wear out in as little as a month or two. When they are not replaced, cartons fail to open or slip out of position causing jams or damaged product costing far more than the cost of replacement.

Maintainability

Maintainability is another issue that adds cost to a machine. The cost of plant technician time is expensive. Availability of the technician may be even more of a constraint. Few plants have enough technicians to do all the things they need to. Some machines are designed to be easier and less time consuming to maintain than others. This is a factor that must always be considered when selecting machinery.

Maintainability includes cleaning which all packaging machines require periodically. Machines used for food, beverage, and pharmaceutical products will normally require especially stringent cleaning as well as sanitation between production batches. Cleanability should be designed into every machine to minimize the amount of time required as well as to make thorough cleaning as foolproof as possible.

It often takes the technician more time to find the cause of a machine problem than it does to fix the problem once it is found. In some cases, they never find the actual problem but apply temporary fix of some sort just to get production moving again. Even something as simple as an open enclosure door can take a few minutes to find on a larger machine. Some machine builders offer diagnostic displays that can point out where the problem lies, which saves time in troubleshooting. Those inclined to be tight-fisted on the initial purchase price might consider the optional diagnostic package an unneeded luxury and decline to spend the money. This may save a bit on the initial purchase, but at the expense of excess ongoing costs. In the end, this can be many times the amount saved at initial purchase.

The cost of downtime on most packaging lines is at least $10,000 per hour and often considerably more. When a plant controller objects to spending more money on what they may see as "nice to have" features like diagnostics, it must be explained to them in simple cost-benefit terms. At $10,000 per hour or about $150 per minute, the cost of each additional daily minute of downtime, 5 days per week, is about $39,000 per year. When it is explained like this, it becomes easier to convince the controller to spend an extra $20,000 for the diagnostic display package.

JOE'S SECRET

How much downtime can you afford?

Maintainability is critical

to uptime.

Components will fail and will need to be replaced eventually. Machines should be designed so that when this happens, the replacement is as simple as possible. Even replacement of something as simple as a $200 photoeye can be improved. Photoeyes and other sensors are often supplied with preattached wiring. This may save a dollar or two, but when they need to be replaced, the wiring has to be restrung through the machine to the control panel. This is time consuming. Photoeyes with a four-pin plug on the body should always be used unless there is a specific reason not to. When the photoeye does fail, the plug is disconnected, the new eye is mounted, and the plug is reconnected. This has the additional benefit of "mistake proofing" the connection. Some plants may have a requirement that only an electrician can connect wiring to a terminal block. If it is a plug connection, a mechanic is usually permitted to do it. This will reduce downtime by eliminating the need to wait for an electrician.

Air fittings are another seemingly trivial component. Some machines almost seem to be built of 1/4" poly tubing. Rather than use ferrule-type fittings that require a wrench to tighten, all fittings should be toolless quick-connect style. This is especially true for any components that must routinely be removed during cleaning or changeover. Operators should not normally use tools, and a mechanic may be required to remove any threaded or ferrule fittings. Making them toolless may allow an operator— after proper safety training—to connect and disconnect them. This frees the technician for other more valuable tasks.

Energy

Most packaging machines do not use much electrical power. A 5-horsepower motor is fairly large for a packaging line, and most are smaller. Many packaging lines use less than 20 to 25 horsepower total. Some packaging lines may use more electricity to light the room than for the line itself. Some may figure that this electrical consumption— compared to other plant energy consumption—is insignificant and may be safely ignored. Even though the energy consumption is low, it should still be considered when selecting a machine. Where more energy efficient motors can be selected, they should be. Additional costs will be offset by lower utility bills even though the difference may be hard to see.

Compressed air is expensive, and packaging machines use a lot of it. (In addition to being expensive, it is often noisy.) Consider how compressed air usage can be reduced. Venturi vacuum generators are convenient, but they waste a lot of compressed air. A small vacuum pump on the machine—or a large vacuum pump to serve an entire line or even the entire plant—may be more expensive initially but more cost effective in the long run. It may be possible to eliminate vacuum altogether in some applications. One manufacturer has done just that with their solenoid actuated suction cup. Instead of vacuum, they use a solenoid to mechanically pull the cup back, which causes it to grip.

Air jets are often used for reject stations or for other machine functions. It may be possible to replace these with mechanical devices that are less costly to operate, such as air cylinders or servomotors.

Shrink sleeves are increasingly popular as primary labels, and the heat tunnels used to shrink the sleeves can use a considerable amount of energy. Where a heat tunnel is required, consider the use of steam instead of electric heaters. Steam may be cheaper and has the added benefit of better heat distribution and shrinkage that is more even in many applications.

Compared to other costs of operating a packaging machine, energy consumption is generally fairly small. Efficient operation should never be subordinated to energy concerns. Within that overall requirement, it is usually possible to find ways to make them more energy efficient. Wherever is possible, it should be done. It may raise the initial purchase price, but the operating savings will usually more than offset the additional expense.

Repair Parts

Many of the components in most packaging machines are not made by the machine builder but are purchased from an OEM. Maximizing the use of standard, commercially available components simplifies maintenance. One example is the PLC. One brand of PLCs is somewhat of a standard in packaging machinery. Many maintenance technicians know how to troubleshoot and program them. Some machine builders may have a preference for another brand. Some may even have their own custom-built PLCs. While this might provide some benefits, the benefits can be quickly eaten up by difficulties in operating and maintaining the non-standard PLC.

This can be a particular problem with some foreign-made machines especially from countries, such as China or India. Components that are standard in these countries may be difficult or impossible to find in other countries. This leads to either a need for excessive maintenance stores or delays in obtaining the proper parts.

Some machine builders discourage their customers from purchasing components from local suppliers. There is some justification to this as it helps prevent customers from modifying a machine by using similar but not identical parts. Others encourage the purchase of OEM replacement parts locally as it helps their customers keep their machines running. Whenever possible, buyers should always request a parts list showing the builder's part numbers as well as the OEM and its part number.

Efficiency

Calculating and measuring machine efficiency is a complex subject and is discussed more deeply in chapter 4. A simple definition of machine efficiency is as follows: how many good products the machine produces versus how many it should produce. If a machine is supposed to run 200 products per minute (ppm) over the course of an hour, it should produce 12,000 products. If, instead of producing 12,000 products, it produces 9,000, its gross efficiency is 9,000/12,000 or 75%.

This inefficiency may happen because of rejected product, machine stoppages for repair or adjustment, a slow machine speed setting or other causes. The key is that the machine did not produce what it was supposed to.

Some purchasers do not pay enough attention to machine efficiency—if they pay any attention at all. This is a serious and costly mistake. Even small increases in efficiency can bring tremendous paybacks.

JOE'S SECRET

Efficiency costs are huge, and are often built into the original machine.

A 1% better efficiency over the life of a machine may save more than the entre purchase price.

Consider the following example with two machines. Machine A is expected to run at 75% efficiency for 2 shifts, 5 days per week. Machine B will run the same schedule but at an efficiency of 78%. The price of Machine B is $225,000 compared to $175,000 for Machine A. The initial reaction may be a reluctance to spend an additional $50,000 for a mere 3 percentage points of added efficiency. When the costs are calculated, it looks like a much better deal:

	Machine A	Machine B
Initial purchase price	$175,000	$225,000
Production rate (ppm)	200	200
Hours per week	80	80
Efficiency	75%	78%
Output per week	768,000	777,600
Output per year (50 weeks)	38,400,000	38,880,000

With its higher efficiency, Machine B, will outproduce Machine A by 480,000 products in the year. Looking at total output, this still does not look like a tremendous difference.

The controller is going to wonder if the difference between 38.4 and 38.9 million products is really worth an additional $50,000, and the controller's initial gut reaction may be "no."

The calculation needs to be taken a step further and monetized. If each product contributes $0.25 to profit (or margin), the additional 480,000 products that Machine B can produce over the year will contribute $120,000 in profits. That will be this year, next year, the following year, and into the future. Every 5 months, that extra 3% efficiency will produce enough extra profit to cover the difference in machine price.

If that does not change the controller's mind, perhaps a new controller should be considered.

This example is rather simplified. Many other factors need to be considered, especially whether the company can sell the additional output. The example uses round numbers to make it easy to understand. That is not to say that it is unrealistic overall; it is not. The point of the example is to show that even small increases in efficiency will generate significant increases in production capacity and bottom-line profit. These increases can often justify spending more money for even a few percentage points gain in efficiency.

This is not automatic. In many plants, the inefficiencies are not so much caused by the machine as by the way the process is run. Unbalanced lines, improper setup, poor-quality products and materials can all contribute to inefficiencies. Even the best machine will not be able to overcome these.

Downtime

Downtime is a major contributor to machine inefficiency. It will be a component of the 83% efficiency in the above example. One major cause of downtime is changeover and—because it is major in terms of total production hours lost—it merits a separate discussion.

JOE'S SECRET

Make sure that all machines are changeover friendly.

The cola bottler in the distant past had it easy. There was only a single flavor in a six-ounce glass bottle to run thus they never did a changeover. The modern plant usually runs several and sometimes several dozen different product/package combinations over the course of a normal week—sometimes even over the course of a day. Each time they have to change from one to another, there is downtime. This changeover downtime can be a little as a few minutes on some lines, but it is more typically measured in hours.

Some packaging machine designs are easier to change over than others. Some machine builders offer option packages such as toolless changeparts or servo-automated setting, which can cut changeover times. Another tactic to reduce changeover times is to purchase additional sets of contact parts so that one set can be in cleaning while the other is in use. These changeover-friendly machines or option packages may cost more than the alternative, and it may be hard to justify the extra expense. "After all," the plant controller may say, "we are only talking about saving 10 minutes a day for this additional $40,000." Ten minutes may not look like much. It takes longer to drink a cup of coffee. What they fail to realize, and may need explained to them, is that 10 minutes of downtime, 5 days per week, over the course of a year, amounts to the loss of an entire week (40 hours) of production. When put into that perspective, it becomes much easier to justify the additional expense.

If the cost of downtime is $10,000 per hour, the 10 daily minutes or 40 annual hours will have a cost of $400,000. Payback on the $40,000 changeover option is less than 6 weeks.

For more information on changeover downtime, its costs, and how to combat it, see John Henry's book *Achieving Lean Changeover: Putting SMED to Work* published in 2012 by Productivity Press.

Residual Value

At some point, the machine will no longer be needed. This may be due to age and wear, the machine may need to be replaced with a higher capacity machine, or the product may be discontinued. The question then becomes what to do with the existing machine and decisions taken at the time of purchase will affect this.

As a rule of thumb, the more customized a machine is, the less residual value it will have. Some manufacturers have been making the same machines for so long that they have become industry standards. At the end of their life, these machines can usually be resold, and some of the investment can be recouped. A custom-built machine, even for a somewhat generic application like capping, may have no value at all, even as scrap. It may have a negative value when the cost of removal and disposal is considered.

The potential residual or salvage value of a machine should be considered at the time of purchase. The weight placed on this will vary with the expected life of the machine. Everyone knows that when a dollar is invested at simple 10% interest, it grows. Ten cents invested at 10% interest will grow to a dollar after 10 years. Less familiar is its inverse, net present value (NPV). The NPV concept tells us that the dollar to be received 10 years from now is only worth 10 cents today. The residual value of a machine expected to be in use for 10 years may not be significant. If the machine is expected to be in use for a shorter period of time, it may be significant and should be considered during machine selection.

The rule of thumb is that about 80% of all new consumer package goods (CPG) products fail. Many times, they fail after their production machinery has been purchased and installed. Sometimes they fail after the machinery has been purchased but before it has been delivered. This risk needs to be factored into the buying process. This is especially true if the product or package is unusual and requires a highly customized machine. If a new flavor of beans is to be packaged in a standard-size can, the risk in purchasing the can seamer is somewhat lower than if a customized cartoning machine needs to be designed and built for a new five-sided candy carton.

One strategy to mitigate this failure risk with a new package is to begin with a semi-automatic machine, using lower speed, standard, machinery. In many cases, it may be possible to rent the machinery. This will result in high operating costs, but these are offset by the lower purchase cost as well as the higher residual value when the machine needs to be disposed of. Once the product has proven itself in the marketplace and production forecasting is something more than a guess, an automated line may be purchased.

FINANCIAL EVALUATION

It can be difficult evaluating competing offers. One machine costs $100,000 but has a residual or salvage value of $40,000 and maintenance costs of $10,000 per year. Another machine costs $125,000 but has a residual value of $60,000 and maintenance costs of $12,000 per year. It seems like comparing apples and oranges.

Fortunately, there are some standard financial techniques for comparing these apples and oranges.

Payback Method

Payback is the simplest of commonly used financial evaluations. It is not particularly sophisticated, but it is easy to calculate. Payback simply compares the expected cost of an investment to the expected saving or other monetary return. Consider the cost of upgrading a labeling operation done by hand with an automated labeling machine.

The cost of the operator is $25,000 per year.

The automated labeler will save 80% of an operator with 20% of an operator still required to tend the labeler. Annual savings will thus be $20,000.

The cost of the labeler is taken to be $30,000. This must include the machine cost as well as shipping, installation and any other costs.

The cost of the investment is divided by the return (savings) to give the time, in years, that it will take to recover the investment:

$$\$30,000/\$20,000 = 1.5 \text{ years or 18 months}$$

The benefit to the payback method is its simplicity. It will give a quick indication of return and can be done on the back of an envelope. It is particularly useful as an initial reality check for a project.

The drawback to this method is also its simplicity. It cannot handle investment or return flows that vary from year to year. It cannot address the expected life of the project. In the example above, if the labeler will no longer be needed after one year, the project loss would be $10,000 less any residual value and there would be no payback at all.

NPV Analysis of Life Cycle Cost

The following is an NPV analysis of two alternative machines. Machine #1 is state of the art and fully automatic, requiring only 1 operator per shift. Machine #2 is a simpler, more manual machine requiring 2 operators per shift. The cost of each operator is assumed to be $25,000 per year. Annual maintenance and running costs for both machines are assumed to be 20% of initial cost. The "interest" cost on both machines is assumed to be 10%. Residual value on both machines is assumed to be the same. This is so even though Machine #2 had an initial cost of half of Machine #1. The reason for this is that the simpler, more standard machine will have a larger pool of potential buyers than the more customized, less flexible Machine #1.

Assumptions	Machine #1	Machine #2
Cost of capital	10%	10%
Purchase price	($200,000)	($100,000)
Installation (25% of price)	($50,000)	($25,000)
Residual value (3 years)	$50,000	$50,000
Residual value (10 years)	$25,000	$25,000

($) Denotes cash outflow or negative value

Net Present Value Analysis – 3 years

Year	Outlay/income	Machine#1	Machine #2
0	Purchase & Install	($250,000)	($125,000)
1	Operating cost	($90,000)	(120,000)
2	Operating cost	($90,000)	(120,000)
3	Operating cost	($90,000)	(120,000)
3	Residual Value	$50,000	$50,000
	NPV	($396,592)	($350,779)

Net Present Value Analysis – 10 years

Year	Outlay/income	Machine#1	Machine #2
0	Purchase & Install	($250,000)	($125,000)
1	Operating cost	($90,000)	(120,000)
2	Operating cost	($90,000)	(120,000)
3	Operating cost	($90,000)	(120,000)
4	Operating cost	($90,000)	(120,000)
5	Operating cost	($90,000)	(120,000)
6	Operating cost	($90,000)	(120,000)
7	Operating cost	($90,000)	(120,000)
8	Operating cost	($90,000)	(120,000)
9	Operating cost	($90,000)	(120,000)
10	Operating cost	($90,000)	(120,000)
10	Residual value	$25,000	$25,000
	NPV	($721,248)	($775,190)

The NPV is the time-adjusted value of the outflows (purchase, installation, and operation) and the inflows (residual or resale value). In the first calculation, assuming a 3-year project life, the net present value of Machine #2 is less negative (greater) than of Machine #1, which indicates that the overall cost of Machine #2 will be less even though the operating cost is higher.

In the second example, assuming a 10-year project life, the decreased operating costs catch up, and the overall cost of Machine #1 is less than the cost of Machine #2.

The question now becomes, What is the expected life of the product? If the product is expected to be obsolete in 3 years, the more manual, lower cost, Machine #2 should be selected. If there is a high degree of confidence that the product will last 10 years, then Machine #1 should be selected.

NPV analysis is easily done using a spreadsheet program. Once the cash outflows and inflows are listed, the built-in NPV formula is applied. The more difficult part is forecasting what the costs will be 5 years in the future.

Net present value must never be the sole deciding factor. Other factors must be considered, including whether the skills to maintain the more sophisticated Machine #1 exist in the plant, whether qualified operators are available to run Machine #2, whether the nature of the product requires automation, and much more. NPV is a useful tool to help compare the total cost of various alternatives.

Internal Rate of Return (IRR)

Another technique for financial evaluation is internal rate of return (IRR). This is essentially the inverse of the NPV technique described previously. Instead of using a given interest rate to determine values, IRR uses given (or assumed) values to determine an interest rate of return for the proposed investment. The project with the highest rate of return, or interest rate, is the more financially valuable one. This tool is also a standard function in most spreadsheet programs.

ACQUISITION

Purchase

The most common way to acquire packaging machinery is outright purchase. This is a rather straightforward transaction: The buyer gives the vendor some money, and the vendor gives the buyer a machine. Once this transaction has been completed, the title to the machine resides with the purchaser who can do whatever he or she wants with the machine. While in theory they may be able to do whatever they want, certain uses or modifications may void any warrantees or worse. In one instance, a buyer modified the safety interlocks of a laser coder. The vendor refused to provide any parts or service until the buyer paid for a vendor service technician to visit the buyer's site and reinstall all interlocks.

Due to the long delivery lead times on most machines, most vendors will require several payments at key points in the project. These payments are generally nonrefundable if the order gets cancelled before the machine is delivered. One purpose of these payments is to assure that the vendor does not get stuck with a custom machine for which there is no other market. Payment terms will vary from vendor to vendor: by the type of equipment and by lead time. A down payment of 30–40% with order, another 30–40% payment on acceptance—prior to shipping—and the balance due 30 days after shipping is not uncommon. On larger projects, with longer lead times, there may be additional payments required at key milestones in the project, such as completion of engineering drawings or fabrication of the machine frame.

Vendors generally have standard terms that that they ask for on their proposals. These terms may be standard, but it does not mean that there is not some room for negotiation if necessary. The terms may also be adjusted based on the credit worthiness of buyer and vendor.

Installment Financing

Machinery purchases may also be financed. This is similar to purchasing a car on an installment loan. Financing may be provided by the vendor, but it is more likely to be provided by a bank or other financial institution. The financial institution may have a relationship with the vendor, or the buyer may work through his or her own existing banking relationships.

Title to the machine passes to the buyer at the time of sale, but the financing institution will retain a lien on the machine as collateral. If the payments are not made when scheduled, the financial institution will have the right to repossess the machine.

From a tax perspective, the interest payments and depreciation will be deductible as a normal business expense. The payments to reduce the loan principle are not normally tax deductible.

Lease

In some ways, leasing is similar to purchasing a machine on installment payments. The biggest difference is that the title does not transfer to the machine user but remains with the leasing company (lessor). The lessee (buyer) gets the use of the machine in exchange for periodic lease payments. These payments normally are fully deductible from taxes as a regular business expense if the lease is classified as an operating lease. If it is classified as a capital lease, the machine will appear on the buyer's balance sheet as an asset and the lease payments as a liability. The lease payments will not be deductible, but the buyer may be able to deduct depreciation of the machine on for tax purposes.

The classification of leases as capital or operating depends on how they are structured and various sections of the federal and state tax codes. Suffice to say that merely calling a lease an "operating lease" does not necessarily make it so. Expert tax advice must be sought when contemplating any lease arrangement.

Some vendors have arrangements with leasing companies or bank leasing departments. A few even have their own leasing subsidiaries. In other cases, the buyer may work directly with their own bank to obtain lease financing.

Leases are negotiated for a specific time period. At the end of the lease, there may be three options for the end user. They can simply give the machine back to the leasing company, if they have no further need for it. Another alternative is to renegotiate and extend the lease. Finally, the end user can purchase the machine. These terms, including the cost of exercising the purchase option, must be clearly spelled out in the lease contract.

Rental

In some cases, packaging machines may be rented. These are usually machines that a vendor has taken back as a trade-in or for other reasons. Another source of rental machines is used machinery dealers, such as The Frain Group. A rental agreement is similar to a lease in that the end user gets the use of the machine but not the title. In exchange for the use of the machine, they make a periodic payment—usually monthly—to the renting company. While they have the use of the machine, they will also have certain restrictions on how and where they use it as well as certain maintenance obligations.

JOE'S SECRET

My three "R"s:

Renting

Reduces

Risk

Rental payments are normally fully tax deductible from income as a business expense.

The main difference between a lease and a rental is that the rental is usually more flexible and for a shorter term. Rental payments may also be treated differently on the user's balance sheet.

At the end of the rental period, the user returns the machine to the renting company. In some cases, they may be able to purchase the machine outright and have a portion of the rental payments credited toward the purchase. This option, where applicable, must be spelled out in the initial rental agreement.

In a few cases, machines may be rented with the rental payments calculated based on use. One laser coding company rented lasers coders with a rental payment calculated based on how many times the laser fired during the month.

TAX ISSUES

Investment tax credits, accelerated depreciation, and other tax benefits may also be available from federal, state and local state tax authorities. These will affect the net price of the machine and must be considered when deciding on the method of acquisition. Tax policies are complex and constantly changing. Expert tax advice should be sought before taking the final decision.

CURRENCY ISSUES

When the buyer and vendor are located in the same country, there are normally no currency or foreign exchange issues. When purchasing a machine from another country, the vendor will most likely want to be paid in the local currency, and the machine will be priced on this basis. This introduces the issue of currency fluctuations into the process. If a US company is buying from a German vendor, the American company will need to purchase Euros to pay for it. The price of these Euros can fluctuate significantly, especially over the course of a long lead time machine. There are ways to mitigate this risk, but they are beyond the scope of this book. Suffice to say that the issues do exist, and when purchasing machinery across different currencies, expert advice must be sought.

There are many costs involved in buying and owning a packaging machine. Price is only one of them. All costs for all alternatives must be carefully considered and weighed.

Nonfinancial considerations must also be carefully weighed. If a machine will not produce a quality product in the quantities required, it does not matter how much or how little it costs. Do not buy it.

Never purchase the low-price machine unless it is also the best-cost machine.

CHAPTER 4

"How Fast" or "How Much"?

When contemplating the purchase of a new packaging machine, capacity is the key parameter. Capacity is a measure of how many products the machine can produce over a given period of time. It is similar to output or throughput but not identical. Capacity is a measure of how much a machine should produce; output is a measure of how much a machine does produce.

Output is what the end user of the finished product is buying, but it is capacity—or the ability to provide that output—that the packaging machine buyer is purchasing.

Capacity must not be confused with speed. A faster machine may seem to have more capacity than a slower one, but efficiency must be considered as well. A machine that runs at 200 packages per minute (ppm) but at 75% efficiency will have less capacity (72,000 products per shift) than a machine that runs 190 ppm rated at 85% efficiency (77,520 products per shift).

SPEED

Speed usually means the actual speed of the machine as measured over a short period of time, typically a few minutes. Speed can be determined by counting the number of products exiting the machine for one or two minutes of steady state operation. The average rate in packages per minute (ppm) is calculated by dividing the number of packages by the observation time, in seconds, then multiplying by 60 to give packages per minute. This is called the "instantaneous speed" of the machine. In addition to packages per minute (ppm), containers per minute (cpm) or bottles per minute (bpm), are often used interchangeably.

When calculating speed, only good product should be counted. A machine running at 200 ppm with 10 rejects per minute is actually only running at 190 ppm output.

Speed is sometimes expressed in packages per hour (pph). This generally means the speed per minute multiplied by 60. This can be misleading as it assumes that the machine ran at a steady rtate for the full 60 minutes. This does happen, but it is likely that the actual output over the hour was less than that due to stoppages or rejected product. Products per minute (ppm) thus seems like the better way to express machine speed.

Speed may also be expressed as cycle speed. A thermoforming machine may cycle 40 times per minute. If it is making 6 blister packs per cycle, it is running 240 packages per minute.

Speed doesn't matter.
Pallets on the truck does.

The speed of some machines, such as conveyors and ink jet printers, is often expressed in linear feet or meters per minute (fpm or mpm). This is a measure of machine speed but not production throughput. If packages are spaced on 12-inch centers (1 package per foot) on a conveyor running at 100 fpm, throughput will be 100 ppm. If the same packages are spaced on 1-inch centers, so that there are 12 packages per linear foot, the same conveyor will have a throughput speed of 1,200 ppm.

When discussing machine speeds, it is less critical how they are measured than that all parties understand what measure of speed is being used.

A machine's speed will also vary depending on the product and size being run. The vendor will usually specify a nominal speed in their brochures or machine manuals. This should be taken only as a starting point. A 24-head rotary juice filler may be rated at 200 ppm , but that is often based on filling water in some specific volume. If the filler is being purchased for to fill viscous juice, the actual filling speed may decrease substantially due to the juice's greater resistance to flow. The vendor's specified nominal speed will also be influenced by the amount of product to be filled. The filler that runs well at 200 ppm when filling quart bottles may struggle to run 100 ppm when filling gallon bottles.

Container design will also affect the speed. The bottle with the narrow neck opening may require smaller diameter filling nozzles. This reduces the flow rate that can be achieved. A wide-mouth bottle may be able to accept a large nozzle, but a high-flow rate may cause splashing and need to be restricted. This too will slow the machine speed.

At first glance, speed may seem pretty straightforward. On closer examination, it can turn out to be more complex. It is important to have the vendor determine the machine speed specification based on the buyer's actual product(s) and container(s).

It seems paradoxical, but in some cases, slowing the speed will increase the output. In a pouch-making machine, heated sealing jaws must weld the sides of the pouch together. Film sealing is determined by a combination of jaw dwell time (the length of time the sealing jaws stay closed), temperature, and pressure. Dwell time is normally a function of machine speed. When the machine runs faster, dwell time is reduced. This may be compensated by increasing the temperature, but then the sealing layer may be too hot and will not solidify as rapidly as it needs to—letting the pouch pull apart before it sets up. Perhaps pressure can be increased, but that brings its own problems as well.

The net result is that when running at higher speeds, there may be a larger number of defective pouches. The machine cycles quickly, and a lot of film goes in but not enough salable pouches come out. Slowing the machine down will allow more dwell time as well as lower jaw temperature and pressure and much less scrap. The net result is that at the end of the day, there is more shippable product and less scrap.

EFFICIENCY

This book talks a lot about efficiency, and everyone will probably agree that higher efficiency is better. One problem is that there are several different ways to measure efficiency.

The basic definition of efficiency is outputs as percentage of inputs. It may be theoretically possible to have 100% efficiency, but for this to happen, there must be no losses in the system at all. In actuality, there will always be losses. Any system that shows a steady 100% efficiency is either calculated wrong or ignoring some of the inputs.

The simplest way to measure efficiency of a packaging machine is to measure actual output against theoretical output. Determining theoretical output can sometimes be a bit tricky, so an approximation may be used.

If a machine is rated at 400 ppm, over the course of a 480-minute production day (single shift) the output for the day should be 192,000 products.

At the end of the day, actual output is counted and found to be 170,000 products. The simple efficiency for the machine is actual output divided by theoretical output or

$$170,000 \text{ products}/192,000 \text{ products} \times 100\% = 88.5\%$$

This is actually a pretty good efficiency, but there are a couple of problems with the measurement:

First, it is calculated at the end of the day. Sometimes it may be calculated several days after the production run was completed. This is like driving a car by watching the rearview mirror. When it is not timely, the efficiency data is mainly useful to berate people for not doing better. It is not particularly useful for reducing efficiency losses no matter how interesting it may be.

One way to improve this is to measure in real time. This can be done manually, but it makes more sense to automate it. Two counters and a clock (typical PLC functions) can be used. The clock increments the target counter by 400 every minute (or 6.6 per second) to give a continuous count of how many products should have been made. A sensor on the machine counts each product made and increment a second counter for actual count. The PLC divides the actual count by target count and sends it to a file or to a screen to display percentage efficiency in real time.

This leads to the second issue. The percentage efficiency above, while helpful, is a gross number that does not give the detail needed to identify and correct problems. There were 22,000 missing products in the example but no information about what happened to them. Perhaps there were 22,000 defective products that got caught and rejected. Perhaps someone had set the machine speed to run at 380 ppm because of material problems or setup error. Perhaps there were no rejects and machine speed was constant, but there were a number of jams causing 55 cumulative minutes of stoppage.

Most likely it was some combination of the three, but the simple gross efficiency (88.5%) does not give any clue what went wrong. Unless more detail is known, efficiency problems will be difficult to diagnose and even more difficult to fix.

Overall Equipment Efficiency

Overall equipment efficiency (OEE) is one tool that is widely used to address this. It is often called "overall equipment effectiveness," but efficiency and effectiveness are two different concepts that must not be confused. Efficiency is about doing things right. Effectiveness is about doing the right thing.

JOE'S SECRET

If instead of producing 192,000 bottles of apple juice, the machine produced 170,000 bottles of cranberry juice (perhaps due to a mistaken production order) its efficiency is still 88.5%. Effectiveness is zero. It did not produce a single "good" or correct product.

The efficient producer will be the low cost producer.

Efficiency is usually a function of how well the operators on the packaging floor do their job. Effectiveness is usually a function of scheduling determining what product to make next. This book will focus on efficiency as it is more likely to be machine related.

OEE breaks efficiency down into three categories: availability, performance and quality. (PAQ, pronounced "pack", makes an easy way to remember them albeit out of normal order).

Availability

Availability is a measure of how much time the machine ran versus how much time it was supposed to run or was "available" to run. There are two ways the available time can be calculated.

Some OEE systems consider available time to be 10,080 minutes per week. That is, all the time, 24/7, regardless of how much time is normally scheduled for production.

Other OEE systems, consider available time to be the time normally scheduled for production. A plant working a 5-day week, double shift, has an available time of 80 hours or 4,800 minutes.

The authors believe that basing OEE on normally scheduled production time is generally a better approach and will use it in this book. More important than the methodology used, though, is that it be used consistently across an organization and that everyone understands what it is and how it is calculated.

Some plants normally continue to run during meal and rest breaks, rotating operators on and off the line. Others plants will routinely stop production. In the latter case, this time should be subtracted from the available time base and not counted against OEE. If there are two 15-minute rest breaks plus a 30-minute meal break, availability becomes 420 minutes per 480 minute shift.

In order to account for all the minutes in the day, time that the line is not scheduled to run should be collected as standby time and omitted from OEE calculations. Some OEE systems call this "excused downtime."

If the plant would normally run continuously, but due to operator absence it must stop production for breaks, availability should continue to be counted as 480 minutes— the 60 break minutes counted as downtime and the reason recorded as employee absence.

Availability = 420 minutes / 480 minutes X 100% = 87.5%

Any time that the line should be running but is not is counted against the availability metric as downtime.

Downtime can occur for a variety of reasons including machine breakdown, jams, no operator, no materials, film roll change, and more. In setting up an OEE monitoring system, it is generally recommended that only the top six to twelve causes of downtime be tracked, and the balance counted as miscellaneous. Too many causes can complicate the system for little additional benefit.

One special case of downtime is changeover, and the authors recommend that it be treated separately. There are two reasons for this: First, it occurs outside of the production run between batches; and, Second, because it is often so time consuming, it represents a significant opportunity to improve availability.

Measuring changeover as a special downtime—especially if major changeover steps such as disassembly, cleaning, inspection and so on can be broken out separately—

facilitates improvement. If a machine has 30 minutes of running downtime, but it takes 2 hours to change over, focusing on improving changeover will probably provide a better return on investment than reducing the running downtime from 30 minutes to 20 minutes.

JOE'S SECRET

In many plants quite a bit of downtime can be traced to imprecise machine setup. This is especially true at the beginning of a new production run. Frequent stoppages to fine- tune or tweak settings are common as are jams and package rejects due to the machine not being quite dialed in.

Another cause of downtime is lack of maintenance. Some plants are so busy that maintenance gets deferred because there is just not time. This leads to a vicious cycle of more breakdowns and even less time to perform maintenance. A good OEE tracking system can help pinpoint maintenance issues and justify getting them corrected.

Use OEE to identify efficiency deficiencies and how to fix them.

Performance

Performance is the ratio of actual speed to ideal speed. The example used here gives the ideal speed as 400 ppm, but where does that come from? As mentioned earlier, for any given machine this speed can change based on the product, product volume, package, machine condition, and other factors. The ideal needs to be calculated for each combination. Normally one will start off with the manufacturer's nameplate specification and adjust from there as necessary to get the ideal speed used in performance efficiency calculations.

Performance measures the average speed of the machine when it is running and does not include downtime. Another term for the difference between ideal and actual speed is speed loss.

In the example, assume that 30 minutes are lost to downtime from all causes, and the machine is actually running for 450 minutes during the day. Theoretically, it should produce 180,000 products during that time. It actually produced 170,000. The performance efficiency is as follows:

Performance = 170,000 units actual / 180,000 units theoretical X 100% = 94%

Performance efficiency should normally count only time that the machine is running. Any stoppages should be counted against availability. As a practical matter, some plants may elect not to track short stoppages that are under a minute or so but count them as performance losses. This simplifies the OEE system and allows operators and technicians to focus on getting the machine running again rather than record keeping. The actual length of stoppage separating performance loss from availability loss is a policy decision. It will affect the availability and performance metrics, but since it will always be captured in one or the other, does not affect the accuracy of the total OEE.

Quality

Quality accounts for rejected products. It is the ratio of products started versus good products finished. In the example, 172,000 empty bottles were placed on the infeed of the line or started in production. At the end of the line, 170,000 good products (bottles) were discharged for shipping. The difference, 2,000 bottles, is the number of defective products. The quality metric is:

Quality = 170,000 good products / 172,000 total products X 100% = 98%

JOE'S SECRET

Quality is the absense of variation.

On many packaging lines, there can be rejected products that can be reworked and replaced on the line, such as a bottle with a cocked cap. An operator may be able to remove the cap and re-apply it by hand or remove the cap and put the bottle back into the capper infeed. Technically this is a quality reject. Since it is replaced on the line and makes it to the end as a good finished product, the OEE system will not count it against the quality metric. Even though it does not get counted in the quality metric, it does slow the performance speed slightly. Thus, it will be counted in the performance metric and captured in the total OEE.

Once the availability, performance, and quality efficiencies are measured, they are multiplied together to give the overall equipment efficiency

$$OEE = A \times P \times Q$$

From the example:

$$OEE = 87.5 \times 94 \times 99 = 81.4\%$$

Overall equipment efficiency is a useful tool because it shows where efficiency losses are occurring. Identifying these problem areas is the first step on the road to improving them.

OUTPUT

Capacity is a measure of how much a machine should be able to produce in a period of time. Output is a measure of how many products a machine actually produces over that period of time. If the machine were running in a steady state with no stoppages or rejects over a period of time, it would be the product of speed and time. In the real world, machines seldom run at steady state for extended periods of time. The machine may stop for making an adjustment or to clearing a jam. It may stop because the downstream or upstream machine stops. It may stop for loading a new film or label roll. It may stop to allow operators to take their breaks or for a shift change. It may stop to allow scheduled preventive maintenance, for training, or for any of a dozen of other reasons.

Even when the machine runs continuously without stoppage, it may not always run at the same speed. Issues with the product, package, or component may require it to be slowed down to avoid rejected products. Viscosity of a liquid product can change over the course of a production day as it warms or cools. Cartons may come from different suppliers: one of which makes perfect cartons and the other of which makes not so perfect ones. Corrugated may have dried out or absorbed moisture in storage, which affects stiffness and how it runs. Every effort must be made to eliminate these variations, but it will not always be possible.

It is important to quantify all performance issues related to materials. How many minutes were lost because the board was not quite right? How much slower did the line have to run because the corrugated was stiffer than normal? Those in the purchasing department are always trying to save money on materials. This is their job and nobody should fault them for it as long as the materials run well.

The classic diffused/concentrated problem occurs again here. If the purchasing department buys less expensive materials, the dollar savings are concentrated and readily apparent. If the materials do not run well, the inefficiency costs are diffused and hard to see. The packaging line has a responsibility to report precisely how much capacity or product was lost because of material problems. A few dollars saved on purchasing may be more than offset by inefficiencies that it may cause on the packaging line.

These stoppages and slowdowns penalize machine efficiency. They should be minimized, but it is not realistic to expect that they can be totally eliminated. Total machine capacity is thus theoretical capacity multiplied by expected efficiency.

Plant operating schedules affect capacity. The plant that runs a 400 ppm line at 80% efficiency for a single shift will have a capacity of about 154,000 products per day. If they change nothing else but add a second shift—perhaps to handle increased seasonal demand—capacity becomes 308,000 products per day.

It should be noted that production on second and third shifts is often less than on the first (day) shift. There are a number of reasons for this: less experienced personnel, fewer personnel, less access to spare parts and maintenance resources, and sometimes just a seemingly perverse desire on other shifts to set machines differently.

BATCH SIZE AND CAPACITY

Many products have a fixed batch size. This size may be due to external physical factors. If making dishwashing detergent, the batch size may be determined by the size of the mixing tank.

In other cases, the batch size may be due to economic factors. There is an economy of scale to batch production due to tradeoffs between costs. Each batch incurs certain fixed costs including costs of changeover, documentation, and testing. There are often losses at the beginning and end of each lot, such as product left in the hoses and tanks as well as leftover components that must be discarded. Other costs include product and components used for trial during setup. These costs are the same whether the batch size is 20,000 or 100,000 products. Running a larger batch size spreads these fixed costs over a greater number of products, reducing their cost per product.

On the other hand, assuming that sales remain constant, larger batch sizes will result in higher inventory levels. This includes greater raw materials inventory as well as greater finished goods inventories. It may also lead to greater work-in-process (WIP) inventories.

Inventory is expensive. There are costs for the warehouse, management, handling, utilities, taxes, deterioration, and shrinkage. The general rule of thumb for packaged goods is that annual inventory carrying costs are about 30% of the inventory's value. A plant carrying an average inventory of finished goods valued at $10,000,000 is paying about $3,000,000 annually in inventory costs.

Another negative effect of large batch sizes is that they reduce a company's flexibility in responding to its customers. If production of potato chips is scheduled to run from Monday through Friday, the company will find it hard to respond to the customer who unexpectedly needs an order of cheese twists on Tuesday. The company will have to carry larger inventories to cover these contingencies, or they will have to tell the customer to wait. Some customers will wait. Others, such as a national chain, may simply shift to a supplier who can better provide what they want when they want it. One such chain accounts for 40–60% or more of total sales for most CPG companies. Not satisfying them could literally kill the company.

SPEED VERSUS FLEXIBILITY

JOE'S SECRET

Slow but flexible is often better than fast and rigid.

High-speed, highly automated machines make sense for proven product with a relatively stable sales profile. This is especially true if the machine can be dedicated to a single product or a few similar products.

The new product with unknown sales volume, the proven product with highly fluctuating sales demand, or the plant with a variety of different products may not be well served by this strategy. They may be better served by slower, more flexible machines that can quickly adapt to variable conditions. In a perfect world, one line running 200 ppm will usually be more efficient and cost effective than two lines running 100 ppm. In the real world, the two slower lines may wind up producing more overall due to their greater flexibility. In the case of a new product—where volume, and even product survival—is uncertain, a good strategy may be to reduce risk by starting with a single, low-speed line then adding a second line as volume justifies it.

Some plants have multiple lines but do not normally plan to run them all at the same time. One distilled spirits plant had seven bottling lines. Normal production volume required only four of them at any given time. This allowed maintenance and changeover access to the lines not in production. When it was time to run the next product, the operators would move from one line to another. This allowed almost continuous plant output.

During seasonal demand peaks, the company would hire temporary operators, mix them with seasoned crews, and run all seven lines.

THEORY OF CONSTRAINTS (TOC) AND BUFFERS

A packaging line can be thought of as a chain of machines. In any chain, the whole is only as strong as its weakest link. In the case of a packaging line, the line is only as fast as its slowest machine. This slowest machine will be the "constraint" to total output. The theory of constraints (TOC), first explained in Eliyahu Goldratt's classic book The Goal: A Process of Ongoing Improvement, says that the way to maximize throughput is to identify the constraint and keep it running at its maximum throughput.

JOE'S SECRET

Find your constraint and keep it fed. Never let it stop.

As an example, a line might consist of a filler, capper, labeler, and case packer. The filler, capper, and case packer can each run 250 ppm. The labeler can run 240 ppm. The maximum line throughput will be 240 ppm, and the constraint is the labeler. There is no benefit to improving the performance of the filler, capper, or case packer. None will improve throughput.

If all four machines are closely linked, any one machine stopping will cause the others to stop as well. Total downtime is not the downtime of any one machine, but it is the product of all downtime. If each of the four machines has a 95% run rate (5% downtime) the overall line run rate will be 95% X 95% X 95% X 95% or 81%. This is 19% downtime for the line as a whole.

Buffers, sometimes called "accumulation tables," can be used to delink machines so that stoppage of any one machine will not necessarily stop the other machines. Buffers should have sufficient capacity to absorb normal stoppages. During major stoppages, they will fill, and the upstream machine will be forced to stop.

If buffers can be used to delink the machines, the overall line downtime will be reduced.

In the hypothetical line above, the throughput constraint is the labeler, and it must be kept running as continuously as possible. The upstream machines must never leave it without bottles to label. The downstream machine must never allow bottles to back up causing it to shut down. Buffers before and after the labeler will prevent either of these things from happening. Because the labeler will no longer shut down due to external causes such as capper jam, overall line efficiency will be determined by the labeler's efficiency—in this case 95%

The line should be balanced so that the upstream buffer is always full and the downstream buffer always empty. The use of TOC to evaluate a line's flow and capacity may show where hidden capacity lies. Better balancing and smart use of buffers may increase capacity without the need to purchase faster machines.

CONCLUSION

The smart buyer will realize that it is only sales that will bring dollars into the company. Sales can only be achieved when there is product to sell. The customer does not care how fast or sophisticated a manufacturer's packaging lines are; all they care about is how much product comes out of the plant and how much it costs. The smart manager or engineer will always focus on maximizing capacity to meet market demand while lowering costs to allow lower prices.

CHAPTER 5

THE PACKAGING ENVIRONMENT

Getting the right answers always depends on asking the right questions. When buying packaging machinery, the questions never end.

The first step of any new packaging machinery project must always be to gather all information about the product, package, components, speed, and capacity requirements as well as any special considerations. If the line is to be installed in an existing space, all details of that space must be known. When developing information about existing spaces, never trust the file information. Verification up front avoids surprises later.

New products generally come from marketing, product development, or package design/engineering departments. Regardless of which department the design comes from, it will almost always be marketing driven.

When developing these new products, the designer may not be fully aware of what is necessary to manufacture them. They may design packages that are more difficult to make than necessary or impossible to make efficiently. In some cases, the first that manufacturing knows about a new product is after the final design has been finalized, and they are told to make it.

A new product or package must never come as a surprise to the packaging plant. They should be involved in the design from the initial concept. Often they will be able to provide suggestions or ideas that allow the product to be made at lower cost while maintaining the market concept.

This is not to say that manufacturing should drive the design. As the adage goes "Nothing happens until somebody sells something" and new products must be driven by marketing rather than manufacturing considerations. It is the final customer who ultimately determines whether the new product is worthwhile or not. Manufacturing will— of necessity—always take a backseat to product marketing decisions. Manufacturing must always have a seat at the design table—even if it is a backseat.

In one case, a manufacturer packaged their product in 5 milliliter (ml) and 10ml glass vials. In selecting the vials, the designers chose two with 0.67-inch difference in diameter. This almost invisible difference in diameter meant that daily changeover took about 90 minutes instead of 5 minutes. This additional 85 minutes of daily downtime cost about 20% of plant capacity. Standardizing diameters would have greatly improved operations with no customer impact.

JOE'S SECRET

If you don't ask questions, you won't get answers.

If you don't ask the RIGHT QUESTIONS, you won't get the RIGHT ANSWERS.

In another instance, a distilled spirits company introduced a new tapered glass bottle. The taper caused the new bottle to fall over as they accumulated against each other. The bottling plant only learned of the new design when a shipment of the new bottle arrived on their receiving dock. The bottle was run semi-manually until a new mold could be made, and bottles with a bottom bumper ring could be delivered. Needless to say, the semi-manual operation as well as the need to discard a complete set of glass molds was very expensive. This is an expense that might have been avoided had the tapered design been shown to the bottling plant at the initial concept stage.

Package designs can impact time to market as well as cost. In another instance, a new carton was designed that was 1/4" wider than the cartoner's maximum capacity. Had the new carton been slightly smaller, it could have run immediately with minimal expense. Consequently, the cartoner had to be replaced with the attendant costs and delays. In this case, if the additional width was truly necessary, some of the delays could have been avoided by advising manufacturing sooner so they could begin planning for it.

In the past, package designers and manufacturing often had to rely on drawings of the new package. These usually provided all the information about the product and package but without actually providing a sample. Once the design was finalized, mockups might be made. The process of making mockups was time consuming and could be costly. This prevented mockups from being created as early in the process as they should have been.

Rapid prototyping technology, often generically called "3D printing," has ended that. Three-dimensional printing uses various techniques to make bottle, cap, or other component samples directly from CAD drawings in hours or minutes. Other prototyping systems that can rapidly print and die-cut custom designed cartons, cases, labels, pouches, or other paper and film components are also available.

Three-dimensional prototypes are extremely helpful in visualizing how the package will look and how it will be produced. A bottle that looks stable in a 2D drawing may prove to be unstable in the 3D prototype. It is better to address these problems during initial design than after they have gone into production.

Sample product should also be provided as early in the process as possible. Liquids that are supposed to be free-flowing may not be and vice-versa. A candy product may have some residual stickiness that makes it hard to handle. These may only show up when samples of the product are available.

BILL OF MATERIALS (BOM) AND PACKAGE SPECIFICATIONS

The starting point in any project is the bill-of-materials (BOM). The BOM must be complete down to the last piece of sealing tape. The BOM should have detailed information on each component and product including size, material, weight, shape, and any special requirements such as temperature, humidity, fragility, or flammability. If this level of detail is not included in the BOM, it must be included in supplemental documents with the BOM.

The BOM, or a supplemental document, must describe how the components come from the supplier. A dispensing cap may specify an overcap protecting the dispensing tip. The machine buyer needs to know whether this is supplied as a single item, pre-assembled by the supplier, or as two separate pieces to be assembled on the packaging line. If the carton includes an internal antitheft tag, the buyer needs to know where it is to be applied. If it is applied at the carton converter (manufacturer) this may cause issues with the cartoner magazine that must be addressed. If the tags are to be applied on the packaging line, this will require an additional piece of equipment on the line.

Cases may be closed with hot glue, tape, or staples. The buyer must know which will be used so that they can provide the appropriate case closing machine.

Some components such as glue or tape may be treated as supplies and not included on the BOM. This is a mistake as it can lead to these components being missed in the project. The BOM must include EVERYTHING. This point cannot be emphasized strongly enough.

Products and components may have special handling requirements, and these must be called out. A cosmetic product may have a highly finished cap that will get scuffed if handled in a normal capper. A product may be light sensitive and require special lighting to prevent degradation. Other products may require a higher or lower temperature and humidity or special air filtration. Still others will be flammable or explosive. Any special characteristics outside of the norm must be noted on the data sheets for each product or component.

DETERMINE MANUFACTURING REQUIREMENTS

As the product and package are being defined, manufacturing should also be working to determine where it will be made. In some cases, this may be a new building or space that can be designed around the product requirement. In many cases, the new machinery needs to be fitted into an existing space. In all cases, there are a number of machine-related requirements that must be addressed.

Capacity Requirements

Capacity requirements were discussed in detail in Chapter 4. Suffice to say that there is little that can be done until these details are known. In addition to the overall capacity requirements, the project manager will need to know if this is to be single or multiple shifts as this will affect the required speeds.

ROOM CONSTRUCTION

Size

The first question is size: How much space is available for the machine or line?

The space must be adequately sized, neither too small nor too large. If the area is too large, it can cause an excess of movement to move between the various parts of the room. An area that is too large can encourage build up of excess work-in-process inventory with all the inefficiencies that this causes and lead to an accumulation of unnecessary clutter.

Floor space is expensive and in most plants, the fight will be to have enough space, not having too much. It is important that there be appropriate access to the machine with space to operate it and work on it. There should be adequate clearance on all four sides of the machine.

Raw square footage is not the only thing to worry about. Rooms may have columns or other obstructions that can limit machine placement. Electrical panel and utility access along the walls will influence where the machine can be placed. Fire and safety regulations require that the machine location not impede emergency egress.

It is critical that the ceiling be high enough to give adequate clearance. In looking at ceiling heights, there are usually two heights that should be considered.

First is the actual ceiling height. This is what one sees when entering the room. In many plants this may be a drop-in tile ceiling or a gypsum board (drywall) ceiling. Generally, it is best to consider this height as the limit when selecting machinery.

Where this type of ceiling exists, there may or may not be additional clearance above it to the joists supporting the roof or the floor above. If there is additional clearance, it may be possible to raise a part of the ceiling if it is required to accommodate a tall machine. If contemplating this, there is no substitute for visual inspection. Murphy's Law says that even if there is space above the ceiling, there will be an air duct or some other obstruction making it difficult or impossible to raise the ceiling.

If there are no obstructions or other factors preventing raising the ceiling, the maximum height becomes the height to the underside of the floor or roof above. It will generally be impossible to go higher than this—though there may be some exceptions. At one company, there was inadequate height for the bulk feeding system for its bottle orienters and cappers. This company put the bulk hopper on the second floor and fed through chutes to the orienter and capper. In addition to solving the height problem, this had the added benefit of removing material handling from the packaging floor.

Ceiling height is not, itself, the critical factor. The critical dimension is the distance between floor and ceiling. One plant knew their ceiling height, and the floor height was assumed to be uniform throughout the plant. That was a mistake.

The filling room had a false floor, raised about a foot as an air plenum. Although the engineers were careful about ceiling clearance, they did not consider the floor height. When a new machine was delivered, it was too tall and had to be modified in the field with great difficulty. It is always a good idea to directly measure the actual floor to ceiling height as well as all other dimensions.

Cleaning must usually be done with the line stopped. The larger the space, the more time will be required for cleaning and the less running time will be available. An important factor in cleaning is ceiling height. Ceilings that are too high mean more wall area. This is compounded by the fact that vertical surfaces are harder to clean, and it becomes even more difficult the higher the vertical surface. Keep ceilings just high enough.

Access doors must be checked to make sure they are of adequate size and location to get the machine into the room as well as to move raw materials, components, and finished good into and out of the room.

Door location can influence the overall design of the line as well as product flow through the plant. If there are doors on both ends of the room, a straight-line layout may be preferred. If doors are at one end of the room, a "U–shaped" line may be better. Location of raw materials and finished goods warehouses will also influence the line layout.

Access

One of the questions that needs to be answered early in the process is how the product and components come to the packaging line. The bulkiest product item usually is the container (bottle, can, jar). There are several ways that the container can be brought to the line, and the way that is chosen will affect both room and machine design. This will also affect the machine vendor selection, or the vendor chosen may affect the way containers come to the line. Common choices include the containers layered on pallets, randomly oriented in pallet-sized gaylord boxes, randomly oriented in smaller boxes or bags for manual dumping, oriented in reshipper or disposable cases, or shrinkwrapped in bundles.

If the containers are packed in corrugated cases, this will generate dust and particulates from handling. It is generally preferable to have the unloading area separated from the filling machine to avoid contamination.

The product itself can also be brought to the line in several different ways including via pipeline or conveyor; movable product tank; drums on pallets; and small (five gallon or less) containers are some common methods.

The buyer must know how all materials come to the line so that proper arrangements to room, line, and machine design can be made.

Floor Loading

Most packaging machinery is not particularly heavy. If located on a ground floor (slab), floor loading is not usually an issue but should still be verified. If located above the ground floor, floor loading must be verified. Each packaging machine may be relatively lightweight. The accumulation of machines may be heavy beyond the capacity of the floor that will be holding them up.

Construction materials

Interior walls may be block, brick, concrete, drywall, plastic, or other. Whatever material is chosen for the walls, smoothness is key to keeping them clean. A rough block or brick wall increases the chance of contamination and offers dirt a place to hide. That same wall can be painted with a heavy, block filling, paint which will render the surface impermeable, smooth and easy to clean.

The same goes for floors and ceilings as well. There are a number of materials available, but the key is to keep them as smooth as possible for cleanliness.

Heating, Ventilation, and Air Conditioning

Most packaging areas should be kept at about 70–80 degrees Fahrenheit (F) and 30–60% relative humidity. These areas need to be adequately ventilated with sufficient fresh air turnover. Some products will require hotter or colder or wetter or drier environments. Dusty operations may require additional ventilation as well as filtration. "Clean" production rooms may require HEPA filtration in order to meet cleanliness classifications such as Class 100 or Class 10,000. The building designer or operator needs to be made aware of the requirement so that they can be met.

UTILITIES

The main utilities required for packaging machinery include electricity, compressed air and other gasses, vacuum, cooling water, and steam. The buyer must know what utilities are available. If these are not available as required, the buyer may be able to choose other machinery—for example an electric rather than a steam heat tunnel. If this cannot be done, additional utilities will need to be installed, and this cost needs to be charged to the project budget. More importantly, it needs to be factored into the project schedule.

Electrical

Electricity is defined by four major parameters: voltage, amperage, frequency, and phase. The buyer must make sure that the electrical requirements of the machine match the electrical supply.

Standard wall socket electricity in the US is nominally 120 volts, 15–20 ampere, 60 hertz, single phase. Some smaller packaging machinery will be able to use this right out of the wall. Larger machines, with heating coils or larger motors use more electricity. If these ran at 120 volts, the current draw (amperes) would be prohibitive. Increasing the voltage to 240 volts halves the current draw and attendant losses allowing for smaller wiring and controls. Increasing it to 480 volts halves it again. Note to electricians and engineers: Yes, this is somewhat simplified.

Got Jiuce?

Make sure the electrical and other utiliy systems can handle the load.

120/240 volt single phase power is almost universally available in the US, but in larger machines 230/460 volt three-phase power will required. Most, though not all, industrial buildings will have this service into the building. If it is not available, it may be expensive to bring it to the building. It may be possible to purchase machines using 240 volts single-phase current. Although these machines will be less efficient to operate, they will avoid the expense of installing three-phase service.

In the US, the standard electrical frequency is 60hz (hertz), or cycles per second. In other parts of the world, 50hz is standard. This can be an issue when exporting or importing machines between countries. If the frequency is different, this can sometimes be corrected via controllers, but it may be necessary to replace motors and other controls to match the local frequency.

Modern packaging machines commonly use sophisticated electronics such as PLCs and servo motors. These are fairly robust, but the electrical power to them must also be clean without severe voltage spikes or drops. In some plants, it may be necessary to provide dedicated electrical circuits, surge protection or other filtering to assure that the power to the machine is sufficiently clean to avoid any electrical problems.

In all cases, electrical supply at the proposed machine location must be verified to assure that it is compatible with machine requirements. If not, it may be possible to adapt the machine. In other cases, modifications to the electrical supply will be required. The earlier this information is confirmed, the better.

Compressed Air

Most packaging machines use compressed air, often to power air cylinders. One mistake some buyers make is to not consider total compressed air usage. The usage at each air cylinder may be minimal, but cumulatively, over a machine, line, or plant they add up. The buyer must be sure that they do not overload the plant's compressed air system capacity.

Plant air pressure is usually in the range of 100–125PSI, and this is sufficient for most packaging machinery. Some machines may require a higher pressure, and in these cases, the buyer must either assure that it is available or arrange to make it available.

Quality of the compressed air is another issue that must be addressed. It must be free from water, oil, dirt, or other contaminants. Any of these will cause premature wear and failure of machine components. Ideally the plant compressed air system should have appropriate filtration and drying at the compressor. In reality, no matter how good the plant air system, it is always a good idea to provide an air station at each machine consisting of a filter/dryer and a regulator. Some machines may require lubricated air. If needed, a lubricator may be added at the compressed air inlet to add the appropriate amount of oil to the air. The air station should also include a lockable dump valve for safety. When closed, this valve shuts off the air and dumps any residual pressure in the machine. The valve is locked and tagged out for safety when servicing the machine.

If the air is to come into contact with the product—especially if the product is for human or animal consumption—further measures will be required to be sure that no contamination can occur.

Other Gases

Some packaging processes will use special gases such as nitrogen to purge and/or pressurize containers before closing. In general the requirements will be similar to those for compressed air. There are two important additions: supply location and safety.

JOE'S SECRET

Remember:
Nitrogen is
a hazardous gas

Where is the supply located? If nitrogen is supplied as a gas in high-pressure cylinders, these may be located in the packaging room near the machine. If so, it represents one more thing to be carried into and out of the room as well as another thing to clean. It is generally preferable to locate the cylinders outside of the room and pipe it to the machine. Nitrogen can also be supplied in liquid form, which allows for more compact storage of larger amounts.

There are some safety issues with nitrogen, and other gases, that do not apply to air. Nitrogen makes up 78% of the air we breathe and is normally thought of as harmless. The danger comes when it is used without adequate ventilation. When nitrogen concentrations rise above normal, it replaces the oxygen on which life depends and causes asphyxiation. If nitrogen is used in a packaging line, nitrogen sensors must be installed to sound an alarm if concentrations rise above safe levels.

Pressure adds another risk with nitrogen. Liquid or compressed nitrogen pressure is supplied at a high pressure, which must be reduced to a safe working pressure. Care must be taken to use appropriate regulators, piping, valves, and fittings.

If nitrogen is used in liquid form—for example in pressurizing beverage cans—there is an additional safety issue. Liquid nitrogen is extremely cold (-321º F) and will cause severe burns on contact with the skin. Whenever liquid nitrogen is present, adequate safeguards must be provided to prevent human contact.

Vacuum

Vacuum is used in many packaging applications including suction cups (suckers) used to pull cartons from a magazine and open them, depressurizing cans or bottles for vacuum packaging, or removal of debris from operations such as hole punching on bags.

Some applications such as vacuum packing of bottles may require a fairly deep vacuum in the range of 28–30 inches of mercury but relatively low flow rate. Others, such as suction cups, will require less deep vacuum, but a higher flow rate. Still other applications such as debris removal require even less vacuum but at a high flow rate. Vacuum can be provided as a central plant or line utility requiring only piping to the point of use. It is often provided at the machine using venturis or vacuum pumps sized to the application. Venturies are inexpensive and, with no moving parts, are maintenance free other than periodic cleaning. On the other hand, they consume quite a bit of compressed air and are expensive to operate. Vacuum pumps are more expensive initially due to their greater complexity, but they can pay for themselves in reduced operating costs.

The buyer needs to be sure that they know what vacuum will be needed at the machine and whether they or the vendor are to provide it.

Chilled and/or Cooling Water

Cooling water is required for some machines. If requirements are not high, this may be provided with a self-contained water-to-air system. The water is pumped through the machine where it absorbs heat, then to a heat exchanger where it is cooled.

Larger systems— such as tanks of product that must remain cool or even chilled or frozen—will require more elaborate cooling systems, usually, permanently installed as a plant utility.

Steam

Steam has several uses on packaging lines It is used on hot-fill packaging to create a vacuum seal: baby food jars are one common example. Steam is piped to the capper and, just prior to placing the cap, steam is injected into the jar, which displaces the air. The cap is immediately applied, and as the steam condenses, it forms a vacuum that pulls the cap tightly down.

In this application, steam is in direct contact with a food product and must be food grade. Normal plant steam seldom is. When product contact is required, it is generally recommended to have a clean steam generator heated by plant steam or electrically. They may be supplied by the machine vendor, or the buyer may need to provide it separately.

Another common use for steam is shrink tunnels for sleeve labels. Cleanliness of the steam is not as critical here as there is normally no product contact. The steam must be clean enough not to dirty the sleeve or package. If the plant steam is not clean enough, a separate steam generator may be required.

Steam can also be used to heat-jacketed product tanks. This application uses regular plant steam and is mainly a question of supply, plumbing, and temperature control.

Dust Control

If the product is dusty, the buyer must pay attention to dust control. Dust buildup is not only a contaminant to be cleaned, but it can also be a respiratory and explosive hazard. Many plants that run dusty products will already have dust-control systems that can be used. Where a system does not exist, portable dust-collection systems may be a viable option.

Dusty operations should be isolated where possible. Dry products, such as a drink mix, will generate considerable dust but only at the filler and capper. Isolating this dust with a small room or enclosure built around the filler and capper will reduce cleaning time and effort.

Fume extraction is a similar issue. Products or processes that generate fumes or odors must have extraction systems to remove them from the room. When requirements are small, such as for a laser coder, a standalone extractor may be located at the point of use. These extractors typically include an extraction fan, carbon filter for removal of fumes, and a series of progressively finer filters for removal of smoke and other fine particulates. Larger fume sources may require more elaborate extraction systems.

BUDGETS

It is never too early to start worrying about money and time budgets. The experienced equipment buyer may be able to give an initial, ballpark estimate when first hearing of the project. This does not need to be particularly accurate at this stage. It can be a "little bit-whole lot" type of estimate. One issue that can occur is that package designers may have no feel for what it will cost to get their new package and product into production. They may come up with the project, initially thinking it can be run on an existing line with minimal cost. On talking to the experienced buyer, they may find that their "simple" project will require substantial investment in new machinery and the "minimal" cost may be hundreds of thousands of dollars. This may cause them to decide that the project is economically unfeasible and should not be pursued.

This initial "flinch test" can save everyone time and effort by filtering out unfeasible projects early on.

As the project is developed, better estimates of what is required along with better estimates of costs will evolve. All project stakeholders must be kept fully advised of ongoing budget developments.

As with cost, the buyer should develop time schedule estimates as early as possible. The designers need to know as early as possible that what they may see as a cheap and quick project may actually be somewhat more complex than it first appeared.

It is not the job of the buyer to be a naysayer—though he or she may sometimes be viewed as one. It is the buyer's job to provide as accurate information as possible at all stages of the project. In the early stages, this information may not be very precise. The project manager may say "This project will cost between $100 and 300,000 dollars and take between 4 to 9 months to complete." If the designers were expecting to spend $20,000–30,000 and be up and running in a few weeks, the project manager's information, even if imprecise, is very useful.

Project budgets must include all factors. The machinery is one factor, but time and money must be included in the budget for construction where necessary along with testing, shipping, moving and rigging into position, commissioning, and more.

WORKFORCE

Quality and quantity of the available workforce must be taken into account. Some areas have a plentiful supply of relatively skilled workers available. Others do not.

JOE'S SECRET

Machines and workforce must be matched to each other. The smart buyer must examine the availability of both the operators to run the machine and the technicians to maintain it. Availability of the proverbial "warm body" just doesn't cut it. Operators are not generally expected to be highly skilled, but they do need some basic skills as well as the ability to be trained. Turnover will affect trainability as well. Plants with high turnover will not be able to invest a lot in training a worker who is likely to be gone shortly. If this describes the workforce available for the project, the buyer should focus on machinery that is easy to understand and simple to operate. "User friendliness" will be high on the list of desirable attributes. User friendliness in this case means that operation is fairly intuitive requiring little training.

Machines must match the workforce.

If the workforce is more experienced and expected to stay longer with the company, a greater investment in training and more sophisticated machinery will be justified.

Technicians such as mechanics and electricians will be required to maintain the machinery, and their skill levels and trainability will be even more critical. Sophisticated machinery requires sophisticated technicians. If these technicians are not available or if the company is unwilling to pay for them, simpler, less-automated machines without all the control and PLC bells and whistles will be more appropriate.

CONCLUSION

Any discussion of what to look for when installing a packaging machine will be incomplete; there are simply too many variables. The issues listed above must be taken as a starting point. Information gathering is an iterative process. The information gathered at the start of the process is may be a bit vague and subject to change. As the project develops, the information will become more and more refined.

The key thing that the smart buyer will always bear in mind is that there is never enough information. The smart buyer will learn to be a "whyner" (not to be confused with a whiner), constantly asking "why?" in their quest for more information.

CHAPTER 6

IT'S ABOUT THE MACHINES

SIX SIGMA

Some vendors will specify machine performance parameters such as fill volume or label placement as plus or minus some value "six sigma." This is related to but not the same as the technique called Six Sigma used in continuous improvement and lean manufacturing. Some explanation is in order.

For any perfectly "normal" (also called Gaussian or bell curve) distribution, the mean or average will always be at the center of the curve with half of all events above and half below average. A standard deviation, called a sigma, is a statistical measure of how close to this centerline events will be. Six sigma represents three standard deviations above and three below the average for a total of six sigma—99.73% all events will fall within this six sigma band.

A process with low variability—such as a filler's dispensing volume—will have a narrow six sigma. This means that all fill volumes will be close to the average. A different filler may have more variability and a wider six sigma.

When vendors caveat some parameter as "six sigma" they generally mean that this parameter will always fall within the stated tolerance but that a small percentage (0.27%) will fall outside, and they will not be responsible for these occurrences.

Accuracy and precision are two terms that are similar and often often used as synonyms. They should not be. The buyer should understand the concepts and how they apply to packaging machines such as liquid fillers. If the target fill volume is 12 ounces, accuracy will mean how close to 12 ounces the actual fill volume is. Precision will mean how consistent the fill volume is. It is possible to have precision without accuracy. A filler may fill exactly 11.75 ounces every cycle. This is precise, but it is not accurate.

Precision is generally preferable to accuracy as it can be adjusted. The 11.75-ounce fill volume can be increased to 12 ounces. If the filler is imprecise, it could fill 11.75 ounces on one cycle, 12 ounces on the next, 11.5 ounces on the next, 12.75 ounces on another and so on. Average fill volume is 12 ounces, but only one container actually contains 12 ounces. The lack of precision often leads to technicians constantly adjusting the machine trying to get it to fill 12 ounces and never succeeding. In fact, by frequently adjusting, they often make the problem worse.

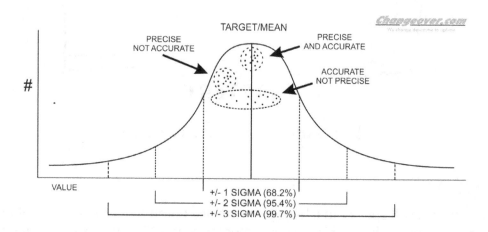

Precision is usually a function of machine design and maintenance. Higher precision is always better but costs more. The buyer must always consider the precision level of any machine under consideration.

CHANGEPARTS VERSUS ADJUSTABLE SETTINGS

Most packaging machines will need to run multiple packages. This means changeover. There are two different design approaches to deal with this; each has its advantages and disadvantages.

Changeparts

One approach to changeover is to design machines with changeparts. Changeparts are product- and package-specific parts that are swapped out during a changeover. A rotary capper might have these changeparts: an infeed and discharge starwheel, a center guide, infeed timing screw, cap chucks, and more. In order to change the machine from a 32-ounce to a 64-ounce bottle, the 32-ounce changeparts parts are removed and replaced with 64-ounce changeparts parts.

The advantage to changeparts is that all adjustment is built into them. This eliminates much of the skill required to perform a rapid and precise changeover. If the changeparts are designed for toolless demounting and remounting, it may be possible for an operator to do it. When operators can do machine changeover, it frees mechanics for more valuable tasks. By making operators more familiar with the machines, it also makes the operators better at their jobs.

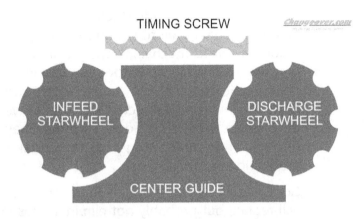

CHANGEPARTS FOR ROTARY CAPPER

The disadvantage to changeparts is also that all adjustment is built into them. Changepart-based machinery requires components and product with little batch-to-batch variation. If the bottles are supplied slightly warped, they may jam in the capper starwheel. If the starwheel pockets are made slightly larger to accommodate these oversized bottles, normal bottles may be too loose and problematic. There is no way to accommodate variation.

A second disadvantage with changeparts is that any time a new product is to be run on the machine, a new set of changeparts will need to be purchased. Cost can range from a few thousand dollars to fifty thousand dollars or more. The changeparts must be custom made, which can take anywhere from several weeks to several months. This will be worth it for the company that introduces relatively few new products and runs them for a relatively long time. This may not be feasible for a contract packager. Contract packagers are frequently making new products and are always under time pressure from their customers.

Adjustability

Some machines, such as inline disk cappers or some inline labelers, are designed to use no changeparts at all. All machine functions are fully adjustable to accommodate any package or product.

This gives greater flexibility than a machine with changeparts. If a plant needs to make a new product, they can turn it around quickly with neither the cost or delay of buying new changeparts.

Another advantage to adjustable machines is that if packaging components are slightly out of specification, it is possible to adjust the machine to accommodate them. Guides may be opened slightly to allow running of the warped bottle that jammed the starwheel in the previous example.

Consider which is more important and choose accordingly:

Flexibility, or

Ease of Setup

The downside of an adjustable machine is that it takes a higher degree of skill to set up for each product. This may require a skilled mechanic—though in some cases it may be possible to train operators. Even skilled operators may not be able to set all the adjustments precisely. This can result in a number of rejected products as well as jams and other issues on startup. Some machines may take an hour or two of fine-tuning to get up to normal efficiency after production restarts.

Good setup sheets along with measurable adjustments will reduce but probably not eliminate this inefficiency on startup.

Changepart or adjustable machines is not an "either or," rather it is a continuum. Most machines combine some of both.

The smart buyer will consider which point on that continuum is best for the company's plant, people, and product when making the machine selection.

CONVEYORS

Conveyors are the bridges between the islands of automation on the packaging line. In too many cases, conveyors are the last components purchased—sometimes when the budget has run out. Conveyors need to be among the first components purchased. A good conveyor system that is properly operated can make the difference between an efficient and an inefficient packaging line.

Conveyor Chain

There are many different types of conveyors used in packaging. Flat-top chain, belt, roller, and vibratory are a few. Flat-top chain is most common and will be the focus of this section.

Perhaps the most frequently used chain consists of molded plastic links connected by metal pins. These are fine for many applications but are not strong enough for long conveyor runs or heavy loads. Metal chains are available to withstand heavier loading. One style is similar to the plastic chain, but it has formed metal links. Another style uses a roller-style base chain with metal, plastic, or special links bolted to it. All strain is absorbed by the roller chain, which has a high tensile strength.

In selecting conveyor chain, these are the key points:

- Assure that the chain has sufficient tensile strength for both normal operation and any overloading that might be caused by a jam. Chain tensile loading is affected by the chain friction so:
- Assure that there is the correct amount of friction between chain and container. Some applications may require a higher friction to force the package into a machine infeed, up an incline or over a deadplate. Other applications may require a lower friction to prevent damaging the package or placing undue force on a machine.

Conveyor Frames

The key design considerations for conveyor frames are rigidity, material compatibility, and cleanability.

Frame rigidity is especially important when the conveyor carries product through packaging machines. Insufficiently rigid frames can flex, vibrate, or be more easily damaged. This can cause problems, particularly at critical points such as at cap or label placement. Some case packer infeeds require a large backlog of product to push the containers into the pack station, and this can create considerable forces and stress on the conveyor. Extra attention to rigidity will be required here.

Frames are often made of sheet metal formed into a "U" shape and bolted together with spacers. These are often painted mild steel, but the authors recommend stainless steel wherever possible. This is mostly aesthetic because mechanically either material will work in most applications. Conveyors do get dirty and stained in normal use. The first time a conveyor needs to be repainted, any initial cost savings will disappear. Stainless steel will not corrode or stain, and it will still look good five years later.

Aluminum—in either plate or extruded form—is used for some conveyors. One advantage of extruded frame conveyors is that they are sold in kit form. The frame sections are cut to length, and other components are bolted on to build a custom conveyor in a few hours. This reduces buyer's risk because if the project dies, it can be reconfigured and used elsewhere.

No matter how carefully a line is run, product will spill on the conveyor. When it does, the conveyor design will determine how long cleanup takes and how well it is done. One style of conveyor that is common in the pharmaceutical industry but rare in other industries is the sanitary conveyor. The frame is formed from an inverted "U" with the chain riding on elevated rails above the frame. When a spill occurs, it falls on top of rather than inside of the frame. This allows it to be easily wiped up without having to remove the chain. When selecting this type of conveyor, be sure that there is a sufficient gap between frame and chain for easy cleaning access.

Transfers

One of the tricky parts of conveyors can be the transfer of containers from conveyor to conveyor. Commonly these transfers are either end to end (or end transfer) or side to side (side transfer) though other types of transfer may be used as well.

End transfers place the ends of the conveyor in line with each other. There is normally a gap of 6 to 7 inches between the flat surfaces of the chains that must be bridged. A "deadplate," usually of thin stainless steel, forms the bridge between conveyors. This must be as thin as possible to avoid tipping the container. In some cases, a series of rollers or even a series of powered rollers may be used instead.

Side transfers place the conveyors parallel and overlap the discharge and infeed by 18 to 24 inches. Ideally the frames are designed so that the conveyor chains are almost touching. If there is a gap between chains, it must be filled with a deadplate. As containers reach the end of one conveyor, guiderails push them over onto the next one. This allows for smooth transfer with no stoppage. This type of transfer is a must on higher-speed conveyor systems to avoid the use of deadplates

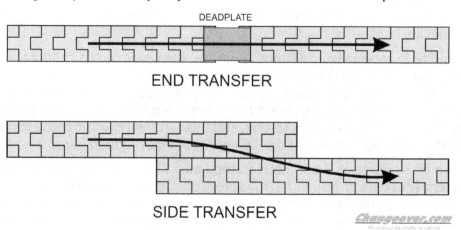

DEADPLATE

END TRANSFER

SIDE TRANSFER

Drives

Conveyors are usually driven by electric motors though they may also be driven by mechanical linkage to a machine, compressed air, or hydraulics. Conveyor drives should always be at the discharge end so that they are pulling the chain rather than pushing it.

It is generally desirable for conveyor speeds to be adjustable. This aids greatly with line balancing. One exception is when the conveyor and machine speeds need to be matched. In this case, a mechanical or electrical linkage will be required to keep them synchronized.

LIQUID FILLERS

In this context, liquid means any product that is pumpable. Liquids can range from low viscosity, such as water, through medium viscosities like oil to very high viscosity like peanut butter or silicone caulk. Liquids can be solutions, or they can have small or large suspended solids, such as red beans in sauce.

The type of filler chosen will depend on the characteristics of the product to be filled, the container, and required speed and accuracy.

There are two major classes of filler: volumetric fill and level fill.

Volumetric fillers measure the amount of product dispensed externally to the container. Pistons are the most commonly used style, but gear pumps, flow meters, time-pressure, and weight-based systems are also in wide use. Each has advantages and disadvantages.

The major advantage of volumetric fillers is fill-volume precision. In volumetric filling, this is usually specified in terms of a percentage variation from the target fill volume. A filler with +/-1% precision on a 12-ounce fill would reliably fill each container within +/- 0.12 ounces (Six sigma). Plus or minus 1% is not uncommon, but for high value products, more precise fillers are available that will run as low as +/-0.1% precision.

Better precision will generally cost more, but reduced product giveaway may make the expense worthwhile. If a product claims to contain 12 ounces, it is necessary to overfill slightly to assure that the volume is never below the claim. If the precision is +/-0.12 ounces (1%), the fill-volume target should be 12.06 ounces. This gives a volume range of 12.0 to 12.12 ounces in each bottle.

The extra 0.06 ounces does not sound like much, but it adds up quickly. For a line running 300 ppm, that is more than 700 bottles of product given away each 8-hour shift or over 180,000 bottles of product given away per year (single shift, 5 days per week).

Level fillers do not measure the amount of product dispensed into the container. Fill volume is determined by the container size and how closely to the container top it is filled. Some common filler types include overflow (pressure, gravity, or vacuum); cascade; and level sensing. Fill precision is normally specified as how closely the filler can maintain this distance. A typical specification might be +/-1/16 of an inch.

If the internal empty volume is stable from container to container, this will usually result in a consistent amount of product in each container. The exception is if the container has a large surface area, such as a can or jar. The filler will still hold the specified +/-1/16 inch, but that will represent much more quantity variation in a wide can than in the narrower neck of a bottle.

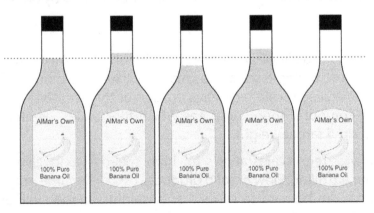

Volumetric fill showing effect of variable container volume

Level filling can be important when the liquid level will be visible on the store shelf. This is especially critical if there is variation in internal container volume, such as what may occur with blown glass bottles. If 12 ounces are filled into in each bottle but the bottle's internal volume varies, the consumer will notice the variation in fill height. Containers filled with a level filler will have uniform product levels and will appear equally full to the consumer regardless of actual product contained. This effect leads to this type of filler sometimes being called a "cosmetic" filler because of the cosmetic perception of uniform volume.

Level fillers are generally simpler mechanically and thus less expensive than volumetric fillers of similar performance. They are available for virtually any speed from low to high. In general, they work best with free-flowing liquids up to the consistency of oils and syrups. More viscous liquids will require volumetric fillers to pump the product into the container.

Liquid fillers are available in rotary or inline or continuous or intermittent-motion configurations at speeds ranging from a few ppm to 2,500 ppm or more. For speeds above 200–250 ppm a continuous-motion rotary filler will probably be advisable. There are plenty of exceptions to this. Speeds of 400–500 ppm may be achievable with some types of inline fillers. One style, the cascade inline cascade- can filler, can run at 2,000 ppm or more.

Another factor will be the container style and product. A non-viscous liquid like a juice in an open jar will be prone to sloshing if it is stopped and started suddenly in an intermittent-motion filler. Even it if would otherwise run well, this might necessitate a continuous-motion filler.

SOLID FILLERS

Solids cover a range of products from fine powders, such as talcum, to free-flowing discrete uniform products like pharmaceutical tablets to chunks like chicken parts.

There are three major architectures for filling solid products. Which one is chosen will depend partly on the product, partly on the container, and partly on the label.

Weight

Weight-based fillers usually weigh the product before it is placed in the container. Combining scales use multiple scales—as many as sixteen or more—all discharging to a single container. Each scale receives a portion of the complete fill, for example, one fourth. The computer then computes which four scales, combined, will total closest to the desired target weight.

The use of many sixteen scales allows for high speeds—as twelve scales can be loaded while four are filling. Flow of solid products, especially large irregular products like chicken parts, can be hard to control, and weight variation will exist between pieces. Some of the scales will be under the target weight; others will be over. The use of multiple scales allows these variations to be averaged out, resulting in a highly accurate fill, even with highly variable products.

Filling by weight works well with all manner of products from fine powders to large pieces.

Volumetric

Volumetric fillers measure the volume of the product either before or as it goes into the container.

Some volumetric fillers use cups of known volume, fill them with product, then empty them into the container. Product-fill volume is controlled by either adjusting the cup size or by using fixed-size cups, which are replaced when changing volume. (See the earlier discussion in this chapter of the merits of adjustable versus changeable parts)

Other styles use servo-controlled augurs (screws) to precisely meter the product. The product is placed in a hopper with an auger in the center. When the fill cycle begins, the augur is activated, forcing a certain amount of product out of the discharge with each revolution. The fill volume is controlled by controlling the revolutions. If each revolution will dispense 3/4 of an ounce of product and target fill volume is 16 ounces, the auger will need to make 21.3 revolutions per fill cycle. One area of concern with an auger-filler is always product cutoff. Some products will flow only when the auger is turning. Others may continue to flow after it has been stopped. In these cases some type of cutoff device will be required in the nozzle.

Count

Some products are sold by count rather than volume or weight. Pharmaceutical tablets are one example. For example, each bottle of a pain reliever must contain 100 tablets—not 1 ounce or 100 milliliters. Hardware items like nuts and bolts are another common example.

Some products may be sold by either weight or count. One popular brand of breath mint claims 30 mints per package. A competitor sells a similar mint in a similar package but claims 1/2 ounce of mints per package. The label claim in this case decides the type of filler.

There are two basic styles of counting filler. One dispenses the pieces single file past a photoeye or other sensor. As the pieces pass the sensor, they trigger a counter that stops dispensing when the correct count is reached. Multiple tracks and sensors—all discharging into the same container—may be used for increased filling speed.

Another technique uses plastic blocks or "slats" with holes. These are often called "slat" fillers and are particularly common for pharmaceutical and nutraceutical tablets. Each hole is sized so that only a single piece can fit into it. The slats are passed under a hopper of bulk product, and the holes are filled. It then moves to the discharge where it is dumped into the container. Fill count is controlled by changing the sets of slats with different numbers of holes.

Density

A key issue with many solid products is density control. Fine powders, such as flour, have a tendency to fluff (increasing volume for a given weight) or compact (decreasing volume). Other products such as sugar can have a tendency to form clumps, which can make consistent flow difficult. It is particularly important when using volumetric fillers to maintain a consistent product density.

Filling by weight eliminates the quantity issues caused by variable density, but density control can still be an issue. Most containers are sized to closely fit the product. If the product fluffs, the desired weight may not fit in the container. This can be a problem with some types of breakfast cereals such as corn flakes. Vibration of the product as it is falling into the bag and vibration of the bag as it goes into the carton can help.

Dust Control

Powders can be very dusty, and good dust extraction is important. One thing to watch out for is an extraction system that is too good. An overly powerful system—particularly if located near where product enters the container—can suck up product in addition to stray dust. If this happens, fill volumes will suffer, and significant amounts of product can be wasted.

Safety

Many fine powders, and some granular products like sugar, can be highly explosive. Whenever working with powders, it is critical that a safety expert review the filler as well as the product handling system and the area in general. Suppression systems and alarms will often be required.

CAPPERS

Cappers come in two main styles: chuck and spinning disk. Chuck cappers use a female chuck that spins the cap down. The chuck may or may not apply the cap as well depending on the machine design. Disk cappers apply the cap in a separate step then use pairs of rotating rubber disks, making tangent-to-tangent contact with the cap to spin it down and tight.

Both styles work well on a variety of bottle and cap combinations. In general, disk cappers will be simpler mechanically than a chuck capper of comparable capacity, leading to lower cost. Disk cappers generally have few if any change parts between bottle and cap sizes. This allows much greater flexibility for the plant that runs many different products or must frequently run new products. Adjustability also makes it easier to compensate when bottles or caps are slightly out of specification. Disk cappers usually require no synchronization at the infeed, which simplifies line balancing. On the other hand, the adjustability does require more time and expertise for proper setup.

Disk and chuck cappers
Courtesy Frain Industries

Chuck cappers generally rely more on changeparts such as grippers, starwheels, guides, and timing screws. These require less skill and time to change, providing more opportunities for operators to perform setup.

Chuck cappers can handle non-round, triangular, star-shaped, and other cap geometries that would be impossible to tighten with a disk capper.

A drawback to chuck cappers over disk cappers is downforce. Chuck cappers tend to apply more downforce than disk cappers, and some bottles may not be strong enough to resist this. A bottle neck ring may allow the neck to be supported instead of all force being on the bottle.

Cap Orientation and Feeding

A critical part of any capper is the cap feeder. The cap feeder accepts the caps in bulk, orients them into the proper position—usually open side down—and feeds them to the cap applicator.

Cap feeders are usually located above the capper and feed the caps down by gravity. This often means that an operator must climb a ladder to add caps to the bulk hopper. No operator should ever need to routinely work above shoulder height or climb ladders or stairs. Floor-level bulk hoppers with elevators to carry the caps to the feeder should be used to prevent this.

One style of bulk hopper combines elevator and orienter. The elevating conveyor is designed and angled so that improperly oriented caps will fall back into the hopper. At the top of the elevator, the caps feed into a gravity chute down to the applicator.

Other styles of orienter in common use include rotary disks, centrifugal bowl feeders, and vibratory bowl feeders.

Some caps may be particularly delicate. Rather than shipping in bulk, these may arrive at the packaging line in trays. Pick and place, robotic, or other techniques may be used to handle each cap individually and to place it on the container.

Feeders must be matched to the caps that will be run so that they can assure proper orientation at the proper speed and without scuffing or otherwise damaging the cap.

JOE'S SECRET

Before concluding that the capper is out of adjustment, verify that the torque tester is properly calibrated and used.

Clutches

The critical function of any screw capper is to apply the cap with a specified amount of torque. Too little and the cap will loosen and leak. Too much and the end user may not be able to conveniently remove it. In extreme cases, over tightening will strip the threads or damage the cap or container.

Whether by disk or by chuck, the capper's clutch must control torque. The clutch must slip or release reliably when proper torque is achieved. One issue the authors see in the field is that cappers are sometimes set so that the wheels or chuck slip on the cap rather than the clutch. This is unreliable and leads to damaged caps, chucks, and wheels.

An alternative to clutches is servo motors. Servo motors can be controlled electronically to apply a precise torque and will do it consistently every time. Another advantage to servo motors is that they can measure and record how much torque was applied to every cap. This allows them to reject bottles with caps that do not tighten properly. As every cap torque is recorded, they can also be plotted onto a statistical process control (SPC) chart for better quality assurance.

Bottle Gripping

No matter how well the chuck or disks work, if the container is not held properly, it can spin, which defeats the entire purpose of controlled torque. Containers must be held— either by side belts or grippers—tightly enough to prevent spinning. On the other hand, they must not be held so tightly as to deform prior to cap tightening. A plastic bottle that is slightly crushed before the cap is applied will remain after being released by the grippers. This will lead to problems in labeling and other operations.

LABELERS

The primary purpose of labels is communication between manufacturer and the end users. Labels can also be used for decoration, tamper evidence, bundling, counterfeiting, and theft protection, and more. The purpose of the label will be the main determinant of the type and design used. Most labels come to the labeler preprinted, but some labelers incorporate printers to print the label just before it is applied. Addition of a batch code and expiration date to a preprinted label is common. A number of applications in warehouses start with blank labels and use a thermal transfer to print a unique label with barcodes, graphics, and other information at the time of application.

Labeler selection will depend on speed, product, type of label, and type of application.

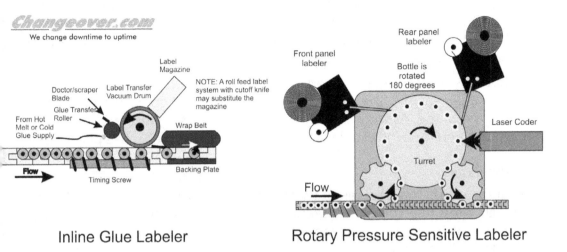

Inline Glue Labeler   Rotary Pressure Sensitive Labeler

There is too much information to do justice to in this chapter, but here are some of the key points to consider when buying machinery:

Label Type

Labels can be paper or plastic. Specialty labels such as hang tags, security tags, and RFID tags may require some special considerations. Standard labels can be supplied on a roll or in stacks of individually cut labels. Roll-fed labels are often supplied with the adhesive already applied and on a backing web. These are called pressure sensitive labels. Roll-fed labels can also be supplied in a continuous strip with the individual label cut off immediately prior to application. Adhesive is applied to either the product or the label as the two are brought together.

A disadvantage to roll-fed labels is that the labeler must normally be stopped when the roll runs out. Multiple labeling heads, automatic splicing systems, and upstream buffering tables can help mitigate or eliminate this problem.

Cut or sheet labels are precut and supplied to the labeler in stacks, which are loaded into a magazine. Adhesive is applied to the label or package just prior to application. A disadvantage to cut labels is that similar labels can be inadvertently mixed resulting in a mislabeled product. If cut labels are to be used, an inspection system to verify the correct label is applied on the product is mandatory.

Sleeve Labeler

Another type of labeler that is quickly gaining popularity is the sleeve labeler. These labels are supplied on a roll, but instead of being flat, they are tubular plastic. Sleeve labelers allow the entire surface of the package, usually a bottle, to be used for graphics.

Buyers should know that there are two types of sleeves:

- Shrink sleeves are the most common. These are heat-shrinkable plastic. They are cut to length and pulled down over the container. The bottle and sleeve then pass through a heat tunnel, which shrinks the sleeve to conform to the container shape.

- Stretch sleeves are also used. These are a stretchable—rather than a shrinkable—plastic. They are cut to length, stretched open, and pulled down over the bottle. As they are released, they shrink to grip the bottle. Stretch sleeves require an indented area on the bottle for most effective performance.

Adhesive Type

There are several hundred different types of adhesives used in labeling, but they can be broken into three categories: pressure sensitive, hot-melt glue, and cold glue. Pressure-sensitive adhesive is preapplied to the back of the label. Hot-melt glue is supplied as pellets that are melted for application. Cold glue, which is actually room temperature, is supplied in liquid form. Each has advantages and disadvantages, but each type requires a different design in the labeling machine.

Label Placement

Labels may be placed on flat surfaces such as a carton or on round surfaces such as a bottle. They may be placed around a corner such as a label that used to seal a carton closed or as tamper evidence on a bottle-cap combination. They can be placed in deep recesses, such as at the bottom of a tube of caulk. The placement of the label must be carefully considered when selecting the type of labeler and specific designs within that type.

Product Orientation

Some round bottles may require no orientation prior to labeling. Others, such as a front and back label, may require no initial front and back orientation but will require holding the orientation once the bottle enters the labeler. Still others may have a feature that is molded into the bottle that will need to be aligned with the label. The first example can usually be run on an inline labeler, depending on speed. The second and third will usually require a rotary label to positively orient the bottle.

Placement Accuracy

Most manufacturers rate the accuracy of their machines as +/-1/32″. This is usually sufficient for most applications, and if the package designers require greater accuracy, it should be questioned. Greater accuracy may be obtainable if required but will add cost and complexity to the machine.

Product Handling

Most issues with label placement accuracy are not due to how the label is placed. Most are due to container position when the label is placed. Product handling to assure that the product is always in the same position is critical. Some products are simple to handle. A full one-gallon bottle is very stable. Others can be difficult. Empty PET water bottles are not only unstable, but they are very soft. Labeling is normally done after filling and capping, but this is not always possible. With empty bottles, special attention must be paid to bottle handling.

Speed

As with any other machine, speed will determine design. There are some high-speed inline labelers—for example roll-through can labelers or inline wrap labelers for beverage bottles. If speeds are to be about 200 ppm and more, consideration should be given to a rotary labeler. Rotary labelers provide much more positive control of the bottle than most inline labelers. As noted earlier, product control is a key to accurate labeling.

While the topics discussed here are some of the more important factors to bear in mind when selecting a labeler, they are not the only factors. As with any other machine, all factors must be carefully considered.

CARTONER

Carton Styles

Carton style will be one of the factors affecting the choice of cartoner. Cartons may have tucked or glued flaps. If the flaps are tucked, they may be reverse or straight—sometimes called "airplane"—tuck. It is important that all cartons be the same style. Glued cartons generally cannot run on machines built for tuck cartoners and vice-versa. Nor can straight-tuck cartons generally run on cartoners built for reverse tuck and vice versa. When cartoners are able to run multiple styles of carton, there is generally a time-consuming changeover process required to convert between styles.

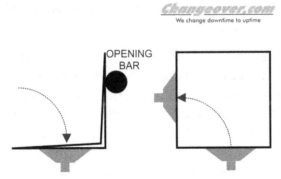

A SECOND GRIPPER MAY BE REQUIRED TO PREVENT COLLAPSE DURING ERECTION OF SQUARE CARTONS

If cartons are square in cross-section, care must be taken with the opening mechanism. The standard cartoner—especially at speeds less than 100 ppm or so—tends to grip a single panel to pass the carton over a bar for opening. Square cartons have panel scores directly opposite each other and, instead of opening, the carton may want to fold itself into an "L" shape. In this situation, a second set of opening grippers must be used to positively open the carton before placing into the chain lugs.

Special cartons such as fifth panel, trapezoidal, and other custom designs will require more attention to carton design.

Most cartons are made of paperboard, but some are made of plastic. Physically these are similar to the paperboard carton and will usually run on the same machines. One issue with plastic cartons is that they may be stiffer, making them harder to open. Once open, the extra stiffness may also prevent them from holding their shape. These issues are usually not difficult to address but do need to be recognized.

Special features on otherwise standard cartons can cause issues. Internal partitions or cut-out panels—with or without film windows—can make the carton more or less rigid then normal and may require some special handling.

Heavy embossing, windows, and perforations can cause issues with the suction cups, which grip and open the carton. If they cannot get a good grip as they pull the carton from the magazine, the carton will slip out of position and jam.

Orientation

Most cartoners are classified as either vertical or horizontal. A vertical cartoner orients the carton with the open ends at the top and bottom. A horizontal cartoner orients the carton with the open ends horizontal. In both cases, the carton is normally oriented with the ends perpendicular to carton flow through the machine. Both styles of cartoner are similar mechanically in terms of how they open the carton, present it for loading, and close it. Vertical cartoners tend to be more common in lower speed (less than 150 ppm) applications than horizontal cartoners. This is a very general statement with many exceptions.

For relatively standard carton formats, the product and loading method will be the main determinants for choosing a vertical or horizontal cartoner. Many products will run on either, but some will require one or the other. Loose jelly beans, if they could be loaded at all, would fall out of a horizontal carton. Some products such as a bottle of cough syrup can easily be hand dropped into a vertical carton. If multiple products need to be cartoned, several operators may be used: one dropping the bottle, the next inserting a leaflet, and a third placing an eyedropper.

Bags of corn flakes, when handled vertically, will tend to bulge as the product settles. This may make the product difficult to fit into a vertical carton. If they are handled horizontally, they will be more uniform in shape and more easily loaded.

If the loading is automated, horizontal cartoners often work better. The bag, bottle or other components are placed into a bucket moving parallel to the carton. They are pushed in and the carton is sealed. As the bucket is open and loaded from the top rather than the end, timing and dispensing is much easier than trying to hit the carton opening.

CASE ERECTOR-PACKER-CLOSER

Case packing is a catchall term often used to cover three different operations: erecting, packing, and loading of RSCs (regular slotted cases) and similar knocked-down cases. Each operation may be performed on a separate machine or as multiple operations—such as erecting and packing or even erecting, packing, and sealing—on a single machine.

These operations are normally carried out on corrugated board, but some cases are supplied in a fluted plastic material. This is similar to corrugated board in how it is handled, but it may be a little stiffer and, due to plastic memory, may want to collapse after opening. This is generally not a big issue, but the vendor needs to know what kind of material the cases will be so the machine can be tweaked if necessary to handle the cases.

Case Erecting

The first stage of the process is case erecting. Case erecting takes the knocked-down case from a magazine, opens the case, and folds the bottom minor and major flaps closed. Case erectors may or may not seal the bottom flaps. It is generally not necessary at this point if tape is being used to seal the case bottom as this can be applied after loading. If the flaps are being glued or stapled closed, it may be difficult to do this after loading, so it should generally be done during erection.

Cases may be erected either horizontally or vertically (open side up). The orientation can depend on speed: higher speeds are often run horizontally, required orientation in the packer and/or vendor's design preferences. Unless product loading will be done on the erector, it is easy enough to convert the orientation of the erected case that it does not make much difference.

Most cases are RSC style, and most case erectors are designed to run these. Some products may require case styles such as overlapping flaps. Whenever the case is not RSC, it is critical to make sure the vendor realizes this.

Packing or Loading

Cases are often packed by hand. Several companies make case sealers with manual case packing stations that are useful when the case is simple, and speeds are low. The operator manually opens the case and places it in a fixture at the infeed to the case top and bottom sealer. This fixture closes the bottom flaps and holds the case in position for hand loading. After loading, the operator manually closes the top flaps and pushes the case into the sealer. A conveyor carries it through, taping the top and bottom flaps closed.

Automated case packing is most commonly performed in one of three ways:

- Drop packers: Drop packing works well with products such as bottles that are packed in a single layer in the case. A complete pattern of bottles—4X3 for a 12 pack or other patterns for other packages—is positioned above the case conveyor. An erected case is staged under the bottles, the gate is opened and the bottles drop by gravity, through guides, into the case. Most case packers raise the case prior to dropping to minimize the drop distance.

Drop packers work well with many packages but do have some limitations. If the product is fragile, it may cause damage. Lightweight products may not fall smoothly into the case, causing jams. Cartons or similar products can act like a piston as they fall creating an air cushion. This prevents them from falling smoothly and results in jams.

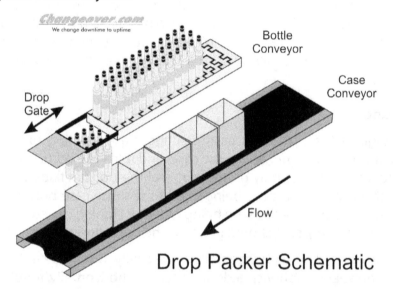

Drop Packer Schematic

- Side-load packers: Side load packers collate the complete pack pattern in a staging area at the packer. A 24 pack might be 4X3X2 (2 layers in the case). An empty case is positioned horizontally, and the complete load is pushed in. The bottom flaps are often open at this point to avoid any air cushion effect. The loaded case is then indexed to a closing and sealing station.

Side-load case packers are especially useful for packages that might form an air cushion if dropped, packages that are fragile, or packages that need to be packed in multiple layers in the case.

- Robotic or pick and place packers: Robotic case packers allow maximum flexibility in packing but can be more complex and costly than drop packers and side load packers. The open case and collated product are positioned conveniently to each other. The robot picks up the product and places it in the case. Robots can gently place virtually any product into any case. If there are multiple lines, robots may be able to handle multiple packing stations, reducing the cost.

A pick and place system is similar to a robot in end result but is much more limited in range of motion as well as flexibility to. It picks the product up, moves it over the case, and lowers it into the case. Pick and place systems work well with a variety of products but are generally designed to perform a simple operation and can be difficult to change if the product or case changes. In the past, they have been a good alternative to robots due to their relatively lower costs. As robots become cheaper and simpler, they become more feasible even for low-cost operations and pick and place mechanisms will likely become less common.

Case Sealing

Case sealing seals the cases closed. Top and bottom sealing may be done in separate operations, or they may be done together. Sealing may be by self-adhesive tape or hot-melt glue. Other methods including staples, cold glue, and wet tape may also be used in certain applications. Simple top and bottom self-adhesive tape sealers are inexpensive (starting around $5,000) and versatile. If higher speeds are required, more sophisticated sealers will keep up with any line speed. Certain applications such as fulfillment warehouses may pack in a variety of case sizes. Random case sealers are available which will automatically adjust, on the fly, to a range of case sizes.

Wraparound Case Packers

Wraparound case packers represent an entirely different approach. Instead of opening a knocked-down case, they start with a flat, die-cut, corrugated blank. The product is collated and placed on top of the blank. The blank is then folded and sealed around the product. This has several advantages:

- Wraparound cases use less board than comparable RSC cases. They also eliminate the need for the converter to fold and glue the RSC blank. Both factors reduce the material cost.

- The flat board takes up less space than the formed cases, reducing the plant's inbound shipping cost. This also frees up storage space in the raw materials warehouse.

- Wrapping the board around the product allows a tighter pack and may allow partitions to be eliminated. This simplifies packing operations as well as reducing material cost.

The downside to wraparound case packers is that they cost more, and all that cost must be paid at once. A company starting a new line or product in an RSC case can reduce its risk by starting out with manual erection and loading and an inexpensive top and bottom sealer. As the business proves itself, it can gradually move to automated erection and loading.

SUMMING UP

This chapter's discussion of things to watch for is almost painfully brief and can only be representative. It is meant to illustrate a few of the complexities in selecting the proper machine. The reader will see that is it nothing like buying a refrigerator at the local appliance store.

The smart buyer—having decided to buy a new machine—will carefully determine exactly what the machine needs to do and how. Only then will the buyer begin to research the various machine types and designs available and pick the ones best suited to the needs at hand.

There are many places where this information may be found but two resources deserve particular mention:

- *The Packaging Machinery Handbook* by John R Henry covers the machines and issues raised in this chapter in considerably more depth and breadth.

- The other is the PackExpo trade show. This show is held every year in Las Vegas (odd years) or Chicago (even years). Hundreds of vendors display thousands of machines, many of them operating. Visiting these shows allows the buyer to see machines running products similar to their own. The smart buyer will attend PackExpo every year whether or not they have a current project.

CHAPTER 7

GET WHAT YOU NEED

Specifications are the primary tool by which the buyer communicates to the vendor what the requirements are for a machine. Once accepted by the vendor, specifications are the tool by which the vendor communicates what they have agreed to build. Specifications serve an important, often unrecognized, secondary function as well: They force the buyer to sit down and figure out exactly what the buyer wants. If the vendor never saw the specification, it would still be a useful exercise to develop one. Good specifications can be time consuming to write, but they are absolutely essential to the smooth purchase of packaging machinery.

A specification is a complete description of the machine or system to be purchased. It will describe what the machine is to do (e.g., load a bottle and leaflet into a carton and glue it closed); performance requirements (speed, efficiency, accuracy); construction requirements (materials and finishes); components to be used; documentation to be supplied and more. It can include purchasing details such as the buyer's desired payment terms, currency to be used, warranty, and delivery.

Most machinery purchases are made with good faith on both sides. Even with the best of faith, there can still be misunderstandings, but a good specification can go a long way to resolving them amicably.

A few packaging machines, such as inkjet printers and simple case tapers are standard and available off the shelf, but they are the exception. Specifications for these machines are fairly straightforward and simple. These machines are what they are with few custom options available.

Most packaging machines are customized to a greater or lesser extent. Some are standard machines modified with custom parts to accommodate specific packages and products. Some machines are designed and built from scratch for a specific package and product. Generally, the more expensive a machine is, the greater the need for customization and thus the need for more detailed specifications.

The project manager is usually the one with overall responsibility for developing the specification, but the project manager does not do this in a vacuum. Any department that will have any responsibility for the machine must have input to the specification writing process. This includes engineering, maintenance, packaging operations, package designers, quality, finance, and validation to name a few. Input must also come from the plant floor. In one case, a corporate project engineer had a preference for French packaging machines. At the corporate location this was fine because they had a local representative to provide support. At the plant level—some distance from corporate—there was no local support, and maintenance was difficult. Input from everyone in the early stages can help performance later on by assuring that the machinery purchased is the most appropriate for actual plant conditions.

The most important input will come from the package and product designers. They need to provide detailed specifications for all packaging components as well as the product itself. These must describe everything in detail, including acceptable tolerance for each component. Where possible, samples of the components and product—as it will actually be run—should be provided. It is important to know any special characteristics as well. If rubber stoppers are to be coated with a lubricant prior to introduction to the stoppering machine, this needs to be spelled out. If they are to be dry, this needs to be spelled out as well. Tip: Assume nothing.

If specifications are developed at the corporate level in an engineering group, chances are that a template or standard format for the specifications will arise either by design or habit. If it doesn't, it should. Companies that do not have a standard specification template should consider developing a corporate strategy for specification writing. This strategy should include who is to write them, who is to participate, and the format in which the specification is to be written. This strategy or policy will help assure uniformity over time and between plants. Developing a standardized template with clearly organized and identified sections will help ensure that important items are not missed.

Not all specifications will use all sections of the template. When a section is not required—such as a currency section when a US company is purchasing from a US vendor—the section should not be deleted. Rather it should remain in the document and marked as not applicable. This ensures that the absence of any currency information is by choice rather than by oversight.

Some sections of the specification may be standard verbiage (sometimes called "boilerplate"). If a company has standard payment terms and conditions such as requiring a Dun & Bradstreet report on vendors, this can be developed by the appropriate department and included in the specification template. The more that can be filled with standard terms, the more uniform the specifications will be and the less work the writer has to do. The boilerplate should be used where applicable, but the writer should always have the ability to modify them when necessary.

Legal Implications

A specification—once combined with a purchase order and accepted by buyer and seller—is a legally binding document. It is a contract between the two parties. In the event that misunderstandings arise between what was sought and what was supplied, the specification will be used to guide any negotiations or dispute resolution process.

Writing Style

Specifications are not intended to be a work of literary art. They are expected to convey, as unambiguously as possible, the desired information. The style must be kept as simple as possible but no simpler. The four Cs of writing can help:

- Clarity: Use proper grammar and precise words to avoid ambiguity. Do not use jargon or abbreviations as these may not have clearly agreed definitions. Use the active rather than the passive voice in writing.

- Correctness: Be sure that all information in the specification is presented accurately.

- Completeness: Be sure that all information that may be required is included.

- Conciseness: Excessive verbosity leads to a lack of clarity. Keep the language simple and to the point.

Do not use pronouns as it can sometimes be unclear what the pronouns are referring to. For example, if writing a specification for a liquid filler say "The filler's nozzles shall be stainless steel"—never "Its nozzles shall be stainless steel."

In general do not use the word should. Should is permissive and implies "nice to have" or optional. In most instances shall is the preferred word. Shall means that it must be done to comply with the specification. Should or may are acceptable in some usages where the vendor is being given some latitude to specify an approach. For example, the specification could say "All photoeyes should be Acme brand (preferred) or Zenith brand. Vendor may substitute other equal photoeyes with prior buyer approval."

TYPES OF SPECIFICATION

There are two main schools of thought on specifications. One school believes that specifications should focus on the functionality of the machine. The other focuses on writing a detailed specification covering every last detail of the machine's design.

Both approaches have their advantages and disadvantages:

The *functional specification* tells the vendor this:"Build a cartoner that will automatically load and seal a 200ml round plastic bottle and a leaflet into a carton at 250 ppm." It is then up to the vendor to design and build a machine that will do this. They will, but it may be that since it was not specified they build the machine for 480 volt 3 phase power supply, and the plant only has 240 volt single phase power. When the machine does not work out as the buyer expected, the vendor can still say that it meets the functional requirement.

On the other end of the scale is the *detailed specification*. In extreme cases, it will dictate the most basic elements of the machine design to the vendor. Sometimes this may be desirable. In most cases, since the vendor knows more about building the machines than the buyer does, it will not be desirable.

Smart buyers will realize that they are the experts in their products and packages, including components, but the vendor is the expert in the machine. The best approach to specification writing tries to combine these two areas of expertise. The ideal specification tells the vendor what special conditions must be satisfied but then leaves the balance of the design up to the vendor (the expert on building the machine).

What should be included in the specification?

General Description

The specification should begin with a general statement describing what is desired. For example: "This specification shall describe a fully automatic, continuous motion, liquid filler. The filler shall run at a speed of 350 products per minute (ppm) of 6 fluid ounces of water-like liquid into an 8-ounce round glass bottle."

This thumbnail description gives everyone a quick picture of what the specification will now describe in detail.

One useful tool is a block diagram showing inputs and outputs. The diagram for the before mentioned filler will show an empty bottle and product going into the block and a filled bottle exiting.

A more complex example would be a cartoner packaging a two-part hair die. Inputs will be a bottle of dye, bottle of activator, gloves, instruction leaflet, and carton. An additional input—though not tangible—will be a manufacturing code printed on the side of the carton and glue to close the carton. The output will be a single-loaded and sealed carton that is ready to ship.

Organization of the specification is important. One useful tool is the outlining and/ or numbered lists feature found in most word processing software. Numbering major sections and their subsections will be very helpful when buyer and vendor are discussing the project, especially if the discussion is not face to face. Section numbers can save confusion and error by assuring that all parties to the discussion are talking about the same section. Use of the outline feature also allows a table of contents to be generated and updated automatically in Microsoft Word and some other programs.

Title Page

All specifications must begin with a title page. At a minimum, this page should include the following:

- Project or machine name (e.g., Cartoner for packaging line #4)
- Project number if used
- Date written
- Written by and approved by
- A table of contents or index must be provided. Depending on style and space constraints, this may be on the title page or may be on a separate page.
- A page header, repeated on each page, should minimally include the project name, revision number, date and page number in the format Page x of y (where x is the current page and y is the total number of pages in the specification). This header, along with section numbers, helps keep the specification pages properly organized.

The specification must begin with a detailed machine description. This must describe exactly what the machine is intended to do:

Provide a proposal for a fully automatic volumetric liquid filler capable of filling 6-ounce round plastic bottles of shampoo at production speeds of 200 packages per minute (ppm) with +/-1% accuracy. Empty bottles will feed into the machine from a bottle cleaner in single file. After filling, bottles will exit single file to a customer-supplied conveyor for transport to an automated capper.

Product Specifications

Detailed specifications of the product and package components must be provided. In the example, this will be the bottle and the shampoo. These specifications may be on separate sheets and provided as attachments. It is important that sample product and bottles be provided as well.

When sending samples, be sure to send disposal instructions as well as MSDS (manufacturer's safety data sheets).

> TIP: If providing liquid product and bottles for testing, it is a good idea to provide caps as well. This allows the vendor to seal up the bottle after fill tests rather than having to leave them open with the possibility of spillage.

If there are multiple products, detailed specifications as well as samples for all products and all packages must be provided to the vendor.

In some cases, samples may not be available. In this situation, the vendor will make a best guess as to what the machine can do but will need to clearly spell out an exception so that the proposal can be modified on receipt of samples if necessary.

Machine Usage

The specification should state whether this is a standalone machine or if it is to be integrated with other machines. If the machine will be integrated in a packaging line, general information about the upstream and downstream machines should be provided. This should include make, model, and serial number as well as details about any electrical, pneumatic, mechanical, or other interconnections with the machine being purchased.

If the machine is in addition to or to replace an existing machine, this should be mentioned. Information about the existing machine as well as comments about what the buyer likes and dislikes about the existing machine should be disclosed. It may also be useful to provide the vendor with specific make, model, and serial number information about the existing machine.

Performance Requirements

Provide the vendor with detailed performance requirements including the following:

- Speed: As discussed in chapter 4, there can be several different speeds that need to be specified. The key speed in this section is the normal production speed. It is best to express this in products per minute (ppm) rather than products per hour (pph). This allows performance efficiency to be addressed separately. Speed will normally be specified for the most critical product with a comment that the vendor shall specify achievable speeds for other products.

- Efficiency: Overall equipment efficiency (OEE) breaks overall efficiency into availability, performance, and quality. Availability is defined as how much time the machine is available to run as opposed to being unavailable due to changeover, maintenance, or repairs. This was addressed in detail in Chapter 3. The vendor should be required to provide a guarantee of quality based on the number of machine-related defective products. This guarantee should be very high—99% is not unreasonable.

   The vendor should also be required to provide a guarantee of downtime from machine jams, breakdowns, and other stoppages.

- Duty cycle: Duty cycle is how many hours the machine shall be expected to operate daily. This may be a single shift (8 hours) 5 days per week; multiple shifts; or even 24 hours per day, 7 days per week, 365 days per year. This last shift is unusual as some downtime for maintenance is normally required.

- Changeover: The specification should include information about how many changeovers are anticipated on a daily or weekly basis and how long a changeover should take. The specification needs to define what is meant by changeover and how changeover time will be measured. This may mean different things to different people.

Functional Requirements

Machine direction must be clearly specified. "Direction" means the production flow, which may be left-to-right, right-to-left, or some other orientation. This is usually described from the viewpoint of the front of the machine. Some directions can be confusing as to what is the "front" or "back." To avoid this confusion, it is always a good idea to provide a small sketch of the machine that indicates production flow using an arrow in and another out, the location of the control panel, and normal operator position.

Running height is normally the height of the conveyor chain above the floor and must be clearly specified. Thirty-six inches above the floor is common—though not universal for many packaging lines. In beverage plants, it is often higher. Running height is typically specified as the distance between floor and conveyor surface. Most machines have some adjustment built in, but it is a good idea to specify a specific target height with a plus/minus adjustment. This adjustment allows for minor height adjustments to be made in the plant to precisely match existing equipment.

Specify how the empty bottles come to the machine, and specify what happens to the bottles after exiting the filler. It is likely that the filler will include its own conveyor, and vendors need to know what their conveyor will mate or join to at the infeed and outfeed. Conveyor transfer types must be specified as well.

Specify how the product, in this case shampoo, will come to the filler. Will it be piped from a compounding room? If so, the vendor may need to provide a supply reservoir at the filler as well as a level control that can open and close a valve to maintain a level in the reservoir. Another option would be for the product to be brought to the machine in a large tank so that no level controls are required.

Construction Materials

The buyer should specify the materials from which the machine will be fabricated. Common materials include aluminum, painted steel, stainless steel, and ultra high molecular weight polyethylene (UHMWPE). When specifying stainless steel, the buyer should bear in mind that there are many different grades. Type 304 is common in packaging machinery, but types 316 and 316L may be required for compatibility with certain pharmaceutical or chemical products.

Product contact parts are especially critical as the product may degrade them, or they may contaminate the product. In the liquid filler, Buna-N o-rings and gaskets might be specified rather than standard neoprene.

Fit and Finish Requirements

The buyer should describe desired machine finishes. These may range from enamel- or epoxy-painted steel to specialized coatings such as Steel-It stainless-steel paint. Aluminum components are usually anodized, but this should be spelled out. If special paint or specific colors are desired, this needs to be spelled out as it may incur

For better visibility:

In dusty applications, use amber colored polycarbonate guarding.

When using wire mesh guarding, paint it flat black.

an extra charge. For stainless-steel components and panels, the degree of polish should be specified. These can range from mill finish for hidden structural components to satin or brush finish to—in some cases— electropolish for exposed or critical components.

Do not ignore the finish on hidden components. The machine frame, hidden behind panels, needs a good protective finish to prevent corrosion. Some vendors will offer an option for stainless-steel frames. This will add to the machine cost but may be worth it in reduced maintenance. This is especially true when corrosive materials are present.

The finish of welds on components can range from very rough to virtually invisible. Rough welds may be acceptable when they are not visible, but they are always a site that will trap dirt and grime and should be avoided wherever possible. At a minimum, all welds—exposed or hidden— must be cleaned and free from slag and weld spatter.

Safety

Some companies will have their own special safety specifications, or there may be special safety specifications by country or industry. Additionally, the product itself will impact safety requirements. The vendor may have recommendations but cannot be expected to know all of these requirements. It is the buyer's responsibility to include them, especially special safety requirements, in the specification.

If a machine is to run a flammable or explosive product, special precautions must be taken in the design, fabrication, and operation of the machine. There are a number of hazardous-duty classifications specifications depending on the product and how likely the product is to be exposed. The vendor will often have expertise and can make recommendations in this area. In the end, it is always the buyer's responsibility to carefully investigate the requirements for each particular project.

At a minimum, machines will need to be properly guarded to prevent operators from getting their hands into moving parts. These may be small, local guards around specific components or may be complete machine enclosures. In either case, all guarding that is not permanently fixed—that is, requiring a tool for removal—must be electrically interlocked. When opened, it must immediately disconnect all power to the machine without cycling to the home position. In the case of a machine with more than a single interlock, it is a good idea to specify lighted interlocks. These will display a small green LED when closed (operable) and a red LED when opened (stopped). An alternative, where the control panel permits it, is to display door and emergency stop status on the panel. This can simplify restarting a machine after a door or guard has been opened by showing their status.

While enclosures are required for safety, they must also provide access for maintenance and clearance of machine jams. Hinged panels should be designed to swing completely open and stay open. Hinges should be of the lift-off type so that panels can be conveniently removed. Some vendors provide clamshell or gull-wing doors that swing up and out of the way for greater convenience.

An alternative to physical guarding is light curtains. These are specialized arrays of photoeyes that, when interrupted, stop the machine. They are convenient and eliminate the need for cleaning guard panels. One objection the authors frequently hear on plant floors is that these are too easy to activate inadvertently. This is just one example of why input from operators and technicians is so important.

JOE'S SECRET

Make sure that all e-stops are easily accessible wherever the operator may be.

Emergency stop (e-stop) buttons should be provided as needed and clearly identified; it is better to have too many than not enough. An emergency stop button must cut all power to the machine when activated. It generally must not cycle the machine to the home position. Generally, an e-stop should be located on the main control panel as well as other locations where an operator or technician might normally be present.

A useful adjunct to the e-stop button on some machines is an emergency stop cable. This is a cable running the length of the machine which, when pulled, executes an emergency stop. An advantage to this is that it is more readily accessible from all parts of the machine.

Lockouts

Lockouts for electricity, compressed air, and any other power source must be provided. When de-energized, they must kill all power to the machine. In the case of compressed air, they must not only turn off the air, they must dump any residual air pressure inside the machine. They must provide a means for a padlock to be applied to prevent activation when there is someone working on the machine. Machines with capacitors and other devices capable of storing an electrical charge after disconnection should have a means of automatically bleeding off this residual charge.

Controls

It is important for the buyer to specify their control philosophy and the part the vendor is to play in it. If the machine is to stand alone, all controls are usually integral to the machine and can generally be left to the vendor (with buyer approval). If the machine is to be integrated into the line, the buyer may wish for the vendor to provide certain control connections, control sensors, or even a complete SCADA (supervisory control and data acquisition) system. Buyer and vendor may have different ideas about how to best accomplish the integration, and these have to be ironed out ahead of time.

Components

All inventory is expensive and maintenance stores especially so. One method for reducing inventory and inventory costs is to standardize on certain brands and models of components such as motors, sensors, or pneumatic components. Another area of standardization is control systems such as programmable logic controllers (PLCs). In the case of PLCs, the issue is not so much inventory as it is the need to use a single programming language on all machines.

Vendors all have their standard preferred components but can usually be flexible in accommodating buyer requests if presented clearly in the specification. Buyers should do this with caution as using non-standard components can result in project delays and additional costs.

If specific components are not needed, the buyer may simply request that the vendor provide a list of commonly used brands of components. This can be helpful in assuring the buyer that all components used by the vendor will be of acceptable quality.

Documentation

The vendor must provide the buyer with appropriate documentation, but the buyer must specify what documentation is desired. At a minimum this should include operating and maintenance manuals, exploded parts diagrams, recommended spare parts lists, electrical and pneumatic schematics, ladder logic diagrams for the PLC where applicable, and vendor data sheets from component suppliers. Other documentation may include training materials and videos.

Many vendors provide their documentation in electronic format on a CD. This is generally recommended, but the file formats must be specified. A common format that works well in most instances is PDF. Any non-PDF pictures and graphics should be supplied in standard .GIF,.JPG or .PNG format. In all cases, in addition to the electronic copies, the vendor must provide one paper copy as well. This provides a reference backup in case there are any errors or doubts about the way the electronic versions are formatted when printed by the buyer

One document that is critical is the setup or changeover sheet explaining in detail how to change the machine from one product to another. If there are adjustments to be made, these must be clearly spelled out for all products covered in the specification.

In the case of some pharmaceutical applications, the buyer may require certain specialized documentation for validation purposes. Although many people, including the vendor, may call this a "validation package" the phrase usually means different things to different people. If a validation package is desired, precisely what it is to consist of must be clearly defined in the specification.

Industry Standards

There are a number of standards-setting organizations that can be incorporated into the specification. For example, 3-A Sanitary Standards, Inc. provides a 3-A stamp for many sanitary fittings and other components, certifying that they meet a defined set of standards for cleanability and non-contamination. If buying a machine for a food or pharmaceutical product, the specification can be simplified by specifying that all product-contact fittings shall be certified by 3-A. The American Society for Testing and Materials (ASTM) has specifications for many piping components, and these specifications can be incorporated into the machine specification by reference.

When referring to these types of specifications, it is important to be sure that the vendor understand what they are. This is usually not a problem in the US, but as more and more machines are imported, it may lead to misunderstandings with vendors in other countries. Other countries will have their own standards-setting organizations and where this is the case, it may be necessary to allow some leeway. The buyer is responsible for verifying that the foreign certification is comparable to the US certification and is acceptable.

Underwriters Laboratories (UL) deserves special mention. Most electrical components used by US machine builders will have a UL certification. For Canada and Europe, the comparable certifications are CSA and CE respectively, and many components may have all three certifications. The UL certification on individual components does not mean that the machine as a whole is UL certified. The one-off nature of packaging machinery precludes routine machine certification. Some vendors do offer UL certification of the entire machine. This requires them to either maintain a UL certification or to bring in a UL inspector to certify individual machines. If UL or other certification is required on the entire machine, this must be must be clearly spelled out in the specification.

Factory Acceptance Test (FAT) and Commissioning Acceptance Test (CAT)

Acceptance testing at the factory (FAT) prior to authorizing shipment, commissioning acceptance testing (CAT) at the buyer's plant after installation, and commissioning will be discussed more fully in the following chapter. All FAT, CAT, and any other testing requirements must be spelled out in the specification.

Training

Training is far too important to leave out of the specification. It cannot be left to chance with the plant operators and technicians simply watching the factory technician during commissioning. All vendors should provide a formal training program for the buyer's team. At one extreme, this can include sending a team of operators and technicians to the vendor's plant and running, changing over, and maintaining the machine in simulated production conditions under the vendor's supervision. Training may include videos, formal lectures, tests, and quizzes. At the very least, there should be a training checklist provided by the vendor to assure that all of the buyer's team has had all the key points explained to them.

How much training and how it is presented will depend on the machine and the current skill levels of the buyer's team. The buyer must carefully consider what training is appropriate and include it in the specification.

Crating and Shipping

Proper crating of the machine is critical to safe transport and must be spelled out in the specification. This will be discussed in more detail in the Chapter 8. Shipping is generally the responsibility of the buyer but may occasionally be the responsibility of the vendor. When it is to be the vendor's responsibility, it must be addressed in the specification.

SELECT POTENTIAL VENDORS

After the specification has been written, it is time to seek proposals from qualified vendors.

Most company purchasing departments will have guidelines on how many proposals are to be requested for evaluation. Three is a common number. It is recommended that multiple proposals be sought where possible. This gives the buyer some different options and approaches. The buyer should bear in mind that the process of developing a proposal costs the vendor in engineering and administrative time. While vendors are happy to have the opportunity to make proposals, as a courtesy the buyer should limit their requests to only those vendors who will be seriously considered.

There are a number of things to consider in deciding which vendors to ask for proposals. There are over 100 manufacturers of labeling machines in the US and several times that worldwide. Selecting just a few for consideration can seem a daunting task.

In selecting, potential buyers should consider the following factors. These are not listed in any particular order of importance—as a factor that may be critical in one instance may be unimportant in another.

- Company or plant policy: Some companies will have prior relationships with vendors. These may be formalized relationships in which the company and vendor have negotiated preferential treatment. Plants may also develop informal practices based on satisfactory past experience with a specific vendor or a desire to standardize brands of machines in use in the plant.

- Capabilities: Many vendors have a particular niche or focus in the machinery marketplace. One company may have a particularly fine reputation for low-speed vertical cartoners for candies. If this describes the buyer's need, they should be considered. Another company may mainly build higher-speed cartoners for household chemicals and have little experience packaging food products. They should not be automatically eliminated, but the buyer must consider whether this vendor will understand the special requirements of food packaging.

- Reputation: Does the company have a reputation for building reliable, easy-to-run, easy-to-maintain machinery? How is its reputation for on-time deliveries? Ongoing support? Companies with bad reputations in these and other areas should probably be avoided where possible.

- Financial strength: Most packaging machines of any complexity are built to order. Delivery times typically begin at 6–8 weeks and extend out to 6–9 months and even longer in some cases. Purchase terms usually require a substantial down payment as well as progress payments. A vendor who is financially stressed may have trouble paying suppliers, keeping employees, and otherwise smoothly operating their business. This can impact promised delivery times. In the worst case, the vendor may fail leaving the buyer with no machine and out the down and progress payments. Even if the machine is delivered, the company may not be around to provide ongoing support.

The smart buyer will carefully check the financial strength of any vendor and assure that they are sufficiently viable for the project.

- Staffing: A company is only as good as its team. The smart buyer will consider both the quality and quantity of the vendor's manufacturing staff. Do they have competent people, and do they have enough of them? This can be especially important with key people such as the project manager or PLC programmer assigned to the project.

- Work load: How much work does the vendor have in the shop at the moment? Nobody likes to turn away business, and some vendors have occasionally promised more than they can deliver. Some vendors have better reputations than others for being able to commit to a schedule and on-time delivery.

- Fabrication facilities: Does the company have facilities to fabricate major machine components or do they subcontract much of this? Either approach can work well, but both approaches can have issues. If they do fabricate in-house, do they have adequate staff, equipment, and tools to do this?

- Testing facilities: Do they have adequate facilities for performance of factory acceptance testing (FAT). Do they have adequate facilities for performing the type of FAT that the buyer wants?

- Documentation: Machine documentation includes operating, setup and maintenance manuals, schematics, PLC programs, exploded view diagrams, video, pictures, and more. The smart buyer will ask to see some typical documentation packages and consider these.

- Parts lists: Virtually all machines have many standard, commercially available, components ranging from air cylinders to motors to sensors. Some vendors will share the commercial part numbers with buyers. This allows the buyer to source parts locally when needed, which is often handy. Other vendors do not disclose the commercial part numbers of components, making it harder to buy parts other than through their parts department. This can be a problem especially with distant vendors. The vendor's parts policy and inventory should be considered during selection.

- Service: The smart buyer will consider the vendor's service capabilities. This includes the quality and availability of service technicians, how long it will typically take for service technicians to get to the buyer's plant and their skill levels when they arrive. More and more, vendors offer distant assistance with capabilities for remotely monitoring and repairing machine functions over the Internet. Some machines have video cameras built in so they can be viewed and diagnosed remotely. This can save the cost of a service visit, but more importantly, it can avoid the downtime waiting for the service technician to arrive.

These are some of the issues to be considered when selecting potential vendors. It may not be necessary to consider all of them in all cases depending on the project. Likewise, there may be additional considerations not listed here. The more sophisticated and the more expensive the machine, the more important they will be. They should certainly be considered prior to selecting the final vendor and awarding the purchase order.

PREVIOUSLY OWNED OR USED MACHINERY

There are many reasons for considering used or remanufactured machinery rather than new. Speed of delivery and cost often top the list. Other reasons were discussed in Chapter 1. If the machine being contemplated is relatively standard, it is sometimes possible to find a brand-new machine, never installed. If a new "used" machine is not available, the dealer may be able to suggest other options that will suit the buyer's needs. Unless there is some strong reason not to, it is always a good idea to speak with used machinery dealers to at least get a feel for what is available.

If contemplating the purchase of a used machine, all of the considerations mentioned for a new machine will apply plus several additional ones. If buying older machinery, it may not be possible to get support from the original builder. The company may have gone out of business, it may no longer stock parts for older machines, or—in a few cases—the company is simply not willing to support a machine it did not sell. To counter this, some dealers buy older machines, disassemble them, and save the parts as replacements. Larger dealers will also have more ability to fabricate or otherwise source obsolete parts for machines that they sell. The larger the dealer, the better they will be able to support their machines with specialized parts and components. Larger dealers will also generally have more and more highly skilled service technicians and shop facilities to provide customization, testing, commissioning, and other technical support.

Documentation is another issue that must be closely evaluated with used machinery dealers. Machines offered for sale "as-is" may have no documentation available. Quality Pre-owned Machinery Dealers maintain extensive libraries of documentation covering virtually all of the machines they sell. They will also have technical writers who can develop additional documentation as required. This allows them to provide complete documentation packages with machines that they sell or rent.

RFP/SELECTING VENDORS/FINAL SELECTION

After writing the specification, the buyer will need to solicit proposals, sometimes known as "quotations," from qualified vendors.

The request for proposal, or RFP (sometimes RFQ), is mainly a cover letter for the specification. Although some of these items may be in the specification, they should usually be in the RFP as well for convenience.

- Brief, 1–2 sentence, description of the machinery desired
- Whether a firm proposal is required or whether at this point a budgetary (sometimes called "ballpark") proposal will do: A budgetary proposal may

be sufficient if the project is uncertain or if the buyer is mainly trying to find out what machinery is available and approximate cost. If the proposal is to be used for requesting funding, the buyer should include a sufficient contingency factor (10–25%) to allow for any cost increases that might occur when the final, firm proposal is requested.

- Contact information for technical and commercial questions: This may be the same person, but there may be a project manager for technical questions and a purchasing or finance contact for commercial questions such as payment terms or currency issues. If they are the same person, this should be mentioned to avoid any confusion.

- When the proposal is due

- Who the proposal should be submitted to and how: Some companies allow project managers to receive proposals, others require that they be routed through purchasing. Delivery by e-mail may be acceptable to some companies, others may require US Mail, FedEx, or other means. If the proposal is to be submitted by e-mail, the RFP must specify acceptable formats such as PDF or DOC.

- If the proposal is to be via sealed bid, this must be spelled out along with the procedure for submission.

- A list of all documents and samples included with the RFP

The RFP should also request that where standard designs exist and meet 80–90% of the specification, they be proposed. There are many benefits to buying a standard design with some customization rather than a highly customized design:

- Cost: The standard machine will likely cost less because there will be less engineering time incurred, standard fixtures can be used, schedules will be more predictable, and the machine builders will be more familiar with the machine.

- Reliability: Any custom machine—regardless of how competent the vendor—will have more problems than a comparable standard machine. This is due to uncertainties in design and the need to work the bugs out of it.

- Delivery schedule: A standard machine will have a shorter and more reliable delivery schedule due to fewer unforeseen problems arising during fabrication.

- Proven machine: A standard machine will have proven itself in use and is a known quantity.

Asking the vendor for a standard machine does not negate the need for them to clearly note all differences between what is proposed and what was requested in the specification.

SELECT THE VENDOR

After all proposal packages have been received, they must be evaluated. This evaluation will examine how well the each bidder is able to meet the buyer's needs. Each buyer, and even each project will have different decision priorities. In some instances cost will be the primary factor. In others it might be delivery speed. In still others it might be geographic location and the ability to provide quick support.

Once all proposals have been evaluated, the winner must be chosen and notified as soon as possible. Ideally they should be notified by placing the purchase order but some companies can take a few days to process the paperwork and, as a courtesy, it is a good idea to notify the winner directly as well as to let them know when they can expect the purchase order, down payment, samples and anything else necessary to finalize the order and lock in the schedule.

As a courtesy, it is a good practice to also notify the losing bidders as well as the reasons why they were not chosen. This helps maintain good relations for the next time the buyer needs to purchase a machine.

Chapter 8 will discuss the process from issuing the purchase order to final acceptance.

CHAPTER 8

THE BUILD

Put simply, the vendor's proposal accepts—with any exceptions—the buyer's specification. The buyer's purchase order accepts the vendor's proposal. If the buyer takes any exceptions to the vendor's proposal, these need to be spelled out in the purchase order.

Once the order is in, there is no time to rest. What comes after the order is placed is as important, perhaps more important, than what came before the order is placed. Now the buyer must make sure that what is being supplied is what is wanted. The specification is supposed to take care of that, and the more thoroughly the specification is written, the better it will do that.

SCHEDULES

When the vendor issues the proposal, it will include an estimated delivery schedule. This will typically be on a condition that it is "based on current forecasts" or similar language. As discussed in Chapter 2, delivery might be 16 weeks today but, if another customer places an order tomorrow, delivery might change to 20 weeks. When the buyer is ready to place the order, but before it is placed, it is a good idea to review the delivery schedule with the vendor. The buyer can say the order is ready to be placed and ask what the will delivery time be if the order is placed tomorrow. This gives the buyer a bit more leverage when negotiating the firm delivery date. Once that date is agreed to, the buyer needs to make sure that all documents, down payments, samples, and anything else the vendor needs is provided on or before the dates required.

Once the order is placed, the buyer should keep in touch with the vendor to make sure that everything is proceeding according to plan.

On larger and/or more complex projects, it can be useful for the project manager to visit the vendor during the fabrication. These visits will often be scheduled around the completion of a milestone but may also be scheduled around the convenience of buyer and vendor.

The purpose of the visit is to assure that the machine is being built as expected. This is primarily to make sure that the machine meets all the conditions set forth in the specifications. In some instances the buyer may find that the specifications failed to address issues that become evident when seeing the actual machine. These should be addressed with the vendor. If changes are necessary, this may require a "change order" changing the terms of the purchase order and specification. Change orders are likely to change the final cost and/or delivery date of the machine and should be approached with caution. Proceed if necessary but only if the benefits outweigh the costs and delays.

If plant visits are not feasible, digital photos or videos may be a satisfactory alternative.

All of the above may be summed up in a single word: communication. The vendor must keep the buyer informed of anything that might impact the machine in any material way. The buyer has a similar duty as well. If anything changes on the buyer's side to impact the project (such as a change in component design) this must be communicated immediately to the vendor.

FINAL TESTING

Once machine fabrication is complete, the final testing process can begin. This takes place in three phases: Pre-FAT, FAT (factory acceptance test) and CAT (commissioning acceptance test). The purpose of this testing is to demonstrate to the satisfaction of the buyer that all specification conditions have been successfully met. These tests may also serve as the basis for the buyer to release progress payments to the vendor. These tests must have been detailed in the original specifications and agreed to by the vendor on acceptance of the order. If not, the vendor will be justified in requiring additional monies for performing the additional testing.

It is important that the final testing be attended by the project manager buying the machine. It is at least as important that the project manager be accompanied by operators and technicians who will be responsible for running and maintaining the machine. The project manager knows about the machine in theory, but the real experts are the people on the floor. Their input in the process and especially in the final acceptance is critical.

There are three reasons for including them:

- If the plant team can do the loading and unloading during the testing, this will relieve the vendor of the need to supply people. This may reduce the vendor's testing charges and help compensate the cost of bringing the team. It also provides valuable experience to the team.

- They are the ones most knowledgeable about how the machine will be used and will be able to catch issues that may have larger consequences later.

- This plant visit and testing represents an excellent opportunity for the operators to be trained by the factory experts.

- When they participate, it becomes their machine, and they will be better motivated to run and care for it properly.

Pre-Factory Acceptance Test (FAT)

During fabrication of the machine, the vendor will conduct various tests to assure themselves that sections or components of the machine are working as desired. These are generally smaller-scale or informal tests for the vendor's information rather than for the buyer. Once the machine has been completed, the vendor does a pre-FAT.

The buyer may or may not wish to be at the pre-FAT. If they can attend, it is generally a good idea. The buyer brings a fresh eye to the machine and may catch things that the vendor's fabrication team might miss out of familiarity. It may be possible to schedule the pre-FAT to take place the day before the FAT allowing the buyer to observe it without the need for a special trip. If the buyer cannot attend, an alternative is to video the trial. This does not need to be anything elaborate, a video camera on a tripod with a good overall view of the machine may be sufficient.

The purpose of the pre-FAT is to verify functioning of the machine without product. It should require the vendor to cycle the machine continuously without product for an extended period of time. Eight hours is typical. Speed during the test should be the maximum-rated machine speed regardless of what the contemplated actual production speeds are. If necessary, sensors and controls may be bypassed to allow the machine to run with no product or package components. During the Pre-FAT, the machine shall be monitored for unusual noise or vibration, excessive heating of motors, interference between components, and any other abnormal conditions.

It is important that the machine run continuously for however long the test needs to be. If there are any stoppages after correction, the test must be restarted from the beginning regardless of the cause of the stoppage.

On completion of the pre-FAT, the machine must be carefully examined. Pay particular attention to metal filings that could indicate metal to metal rubbing or rubber particulates that could indicate excessive wear on drive belts. Assure that no settings have slipped or parts loosened due to normal machine vibration. If loosening is found, the vendor must take steps to assure that this will not happen during production operation. If any evidence of abnormal conditions is found, the vendor must correct this and repeat the full pre-FAT until it can be completed with zero abnormal conditions.

Factory Acceptance Test (FAT)

Once the pre-FAT has been satisfactorily completed, the FAT can be performed. The Factory Acceptance Test (FAT) also takes place at the vendor's plant.

This must take place at the vendor's facility and the buyer or their representative (not from the vendor) must be present. Generally, the buyer's representative should be the project manager who bought the machine and supervised the project. The goal of the FAT is twofold: first, to assure that what the vendor has built is exactly what the buyer, per the specifications, wanted. Second, to assure that the machine is functionally capable of performing as specified under conditions simulating, as closely as possible, the production process. In most cases, it will be impossible to exactly duplicate production. This is especially true with large- or high-speed machinery. A 15-minute test on a 500 ppm machine will require 7,500 products. If the upstream and downstream machines are not present, this will require hand feeding and removal, which can be difficult to impossible. Nevertheless, the FAT should simulate production conditions as closely as possible.

During the FAT, the buyer may notice things that they might wish to modify even though they are in accord with the specifications. This is not uncommon. It will generally be better to make any modifications now—while the machine is still on the vendor's floor—than later when it has been installed and may already be in use.

The smart buyer will be careful about making changes at this point. They should be made if essential but the vendor will, rightly, charge for them. Depending on their nature, these changes may delay shipment of the machine. Avoidance of these last-minute changes is one of the reasons why it is important to monitor the fabrication of the machine from start to finish.

Most modifications made at this point should be minor such as adding another emergency stop (e-stop) and will not affect the machine operation. These should normally not be allowed to delay the FAT but should be addressed by the vendor after the FAT. If significant modifications are to be made, it may be necessary to repeat the FAT.

The first step of the FAT is to review the machine to make sure it is what was ordered. The buyer should check all dimensions to be sure that they are per the specification (and any modifications). Dimensions where the machine must interconnect with other machines are particularly critical. Verify that direction of flow is correct. Check to see that the control panel as well as any auxiliary controls—such as remote e-stops—are where they are supposed to be.

Some of the items mentioned in this section may not be applicable on all machines. There may also be items not mentioned in this section that do require inspection. The following is meant to be illustrative of common inspection criteria, not comprehensive of all cases. All inspection shall be in accordance with the specifications.

Next, check the details of the machine, inside and out. A checklist previously prepared by the buyer can help make sure nothing is missed. Some vendors will provide a checklist. If so, the buyer should review it ahead of time to assure that it covers all areas of interest.

The smart buyer will come prepared for this inspection with a good flashlight, a camera, and a mirror. The mirror makes it easier to see areas that might otherwise be hidden from view. Another useful tool is a borescope with flexible fiberoptic extension. These have gotten so inexpensive (under $300) that there is no reason not to have one. The extension can be snaked into places that would normally be impossible to see. An LED display shows what the fiberoptic sees. An internal camera allows pictures to be stored to an SD card for later viewing or documentation.

Padlocks to lock out all electrical and pneumatic power before inspecting inside the machine are an absolute must-have.

JOE'S SECRET

Always bring your own padlock(s), so you can lock out the machine before inspecting it.

- Inspect the machine internally for proper welds and weld finish. If the welds are specified as ground and polished, they should be nearly invisible. In all cases, they should have been thoroughly brushed (per the specification) and free from splatter.

- Inspect the machine internally for proper finishes. Be sure that all parts are painted or finished according to the specification. Be especially careful to check the areas that may be hidden from normal view.

- Check the outside of the machine for fit and finish. Verify that any paint is smooth and free from any brush marks, runs, or holidays (missed spots). Verify that all doors open and close smoothly and latch and unlatch as they should.

- Any loose components should have shown up during the pre-FAT cycle run, but when in doubt, grab the component and shake it (taking care not to damage any delicate components) to make sure that there is no unacceptable play.

- If component brand names have been specified, such as motors, assure that the component is the specified brand.

Electrical components merit particularly close inspection. Many issues that can arise with wiring and components will be hidden until they occur. Careful inspection of what is visible can give hints to invisible problems.

Some of the things to look for include the following:

- Electrical disconnect: This should disconnect all electrical power to the machine and all of its components and subassemblies. Make sure that it can be locked out with a padlock.

- General appearance of the electrical panel: Is it neatly laid out with enough room for all components? Does it have extra space for installation of additional components in the future if needed? Does it have a 110v ac outlet in the panel? This is very useful if test instruments need to be connected in the future or for the charger of a laptop used when working with the PLC. If one was not included in the specifications, consider asking the vendor to install one now (Expect an additional charge, of course).

- Verify that circuit breakers are properly sized

- Check the wiring: Is power and control wiring separated to avoid electrical "noise"? Is the wiring neatly organized using straight runs and formed corners? Is wiring properly bundled and secured with tie wraps attached to the panel?

- Are all wires clearly identified with printed wiremarkers? Are all terminals—both standalone terminal blocks and on electrical components—clearly numbered and/or identified?

- Verify the machine wiring against the electrical schematics. At this point, some vendors will have working drawings of the wiring schematics with final "as built" drawings to be provided after final acceptance of the machine.

- After completing the inspection of the de-energized electrical components and wiring, close all doors and guards, reset e-stop switches, and activate main power. Test each stop and interlocked door or guard to assure that activation or opening deactivates all power to the machine. Assure that a positive manual reset is required to restart the machine after resetting the interlocks and e-stops.

During this inspection, the buyer should develop a "punch list" of items that are not in accordance with the specification. Some of these may prevent the FAT test run. Others may not and may be addressed after the test run. Once agreed to by the vendor, this punch list must be addressed before the machine can be shipped. The exception will be items that can only be addressed upon interconnection with upstream and downstream machines that are not in the vendor's plant.

The machine is now ready for the FAT test run. This should simulate as closely as possible normal production on the buyer's plant floor. Unless the machine is to stand alone or the vendor is providing a complete, integrated packaging line, this ideal can be difficult to achieve. Ideally, the machine should run at least 15 minutes of production, but this can be difficult if the machine is higher speed or the package is large. The length of the test run shall be agreed upon beforehand between buyer and vendor. The limits of practicality will be the final determinant of the actual nature of the test run.

JOE'S SECRET

If it doesn't look good, it probably isn't.

The vendor needs to have sufficient people on hand to feed the line as well as to remove product from the line at the test speeds. It may be necessary to temporarily install additional infeed and outfeed conveyors and unscrambler tables to permit this.

Once the test is ready to go, the machine is started and allowed to warm-up. The machine may be jogged and/or hand loaded for the initial charge as required. When the first product is fed to the machine, timing begins. The machine will be expected to run continuously with no machine-related rejections or stoppages for the entire duration of the test run. If stoppages do occur due to machine issues—as opposed to product or component issues—the reason for the stoppage must be corrected and the test restarted from the beginning.

If multiple products are to be tested, the vendor will perform a changeover on the machine, resetting for the next test size. The buyer should time the changeover. If changeover times are specified, the timing is done to assure that it complies with the specification. If not specified, it is done to provide baseline data for changeovers on the packaging floor.

It may be necessary to run some products through the machine after changeover to allow for fine-tuning of settings. This should always be as few as possible but as many as required for a proper setup. Once the vendor is satisfied with the new setup, the FAT test run will be repeated.

On conclusion of the FAT, the buyer must carefully inspect the machine for any issues that may have arisen during the run. These and any other issues must be corrected by the vendor prior to releasing the machine for shipment.

CRATING AND SHIPPING

Crating and shipping is critical with packaging machinery. It should have been addressed in the specifications, but, if not, it must be addressed now. If not properly done, damage during shipping can set the project back to time zero. Machines must be securely fastened to a skid or pallet that is sufficiently rigid and that it can be handled without bending or flexing. Generally, the machine should be wrapped in plastic sheeting to protect it from dirt and moisture. Depending on where it is being shipped to, it may also need to be enclosed with a plywood or particle-board crate. If being shipped by ocean cargo, particular care should be taken to prevent exposure to humidity in general and salt air in particular. Desiccant bags in the shipping crate can help.

Larger machines should be shipped in dedicated containers or trailers to eliminate the need for intermediate handling between vendor and buyer. The vendor must assure that the machine is securely fastened to prevent movement during transit. Shock and tilt indicators are recommended to provide evidence of any rough shipping conditions. On arrival, the buyer must carefully inspect the shipping crate for damage prior to acceptance. If there is visible damage, they should notify both shipper and vendor and follow their instructions as well as their internal company practices for acceptance of the delivery.

The vendor will normally have adequate personnel and equipment to load large machines into the truck. The buyer may not. It is strongly recommended that the buyer contract with qualified riggers if they have any doubts at all about their ability to safely unload and move the machinery through their plant. This is relatively cheap insurance to guard against both actual and alleged damage at the buyer's plant.

Whenever possible, the riggers should move the crated machine directly from the truck to the area where it will be installed. It is sometimes necessary to store the machine temporarily, but this should be avoided if possible. Each movement of the machine presents another opportunity for damage.

INSTALLATION

At the final location, the crating (if still in place) and skid should be removed and the machine spotted in its final location. It should be leveled and adjusted to its final running height.

Once the machine is in its final position, all utilities can be run to the machine. Conduits can be run to the control panel and power and control wiring terminated inside. Unless the buyer plans to do the start-up themselves, all electrical connections should be left unconnected as should compressed air, vacuum, or any other connections until the vendor technician is present for commissioning. Leaving them unconnected eliminates any risk of inadvertent activation of the machine before it is ready. In the event of start-up issues with the machine it also provides evidence that the buyer did not activate the machine prior to the vendor technician's arrival.

If final connections must be must be made in advance of commissioning, all utilities must be locked and tagged out to prevent inadvertent actuation.

Integration

Unless the machine is designed to stand alone, it must also be integrated with upstream and/or downstream equipment on the line. This integration is partly mechanical such as conveyor transfers, guide rails, bulk feeders, or reservoirs. It is also electrical/electronic and controls. Some high-speed lines have machines are synchronized with each other using electronic drive-control systems. Some lines will have line-control systems that operate all the machines on the line as a single entity. These are often called supervisory control and data acquisition (SCADA) systems. At a minimum, there must be upstream and downstream sensors to stop the machine in the event of either a backup from downstream or a lack of products arriving from upstream.

The process of making all of these interconnections is loosely called "integration." In some cases, the vendor will be responsible for this, and if so, it must have been spelled out in the specification. In other cases, the buyer will be responsible for it. If the buyer is to do it, the buyer must decide whether to use internal personnel or outside contractors. However it is to be done, it must be completed before the arrival of the vendor's technician for commissioning—at least as completely as it can be. As with power and other connections, it is recommended that control and sensor wiring be run but not connected prior to the vendor technician's visit.

Total or Full-Line Integration

One option offered by some larger machine builders and Quality Pre-owned Machinery Dealers is total integration. At one extreme, the buyer gives the vendor a single purchase order to provide an entire packaging line for a particular product at a specified speed and output. The vendor provides or sources all machinery and assembles the entire line in its facility. At the FAT, since the entire line is available, extended production simulation runs can be made for training of the buyer's plant personnel. Once everyone is satisfied, the line is disassembled, crated, and shipped to the buyer's plant. Once there, the vendor's team reassembles the line and starts it up.

Not all machinery vendors are able or willing to do this. The benefit is that the buyer must deal with a single vendor who is responsible for the entire project. This greatly simplifies the process. The sole responsibility particularly simplifies the issue of who is responsible when the filler and the capper do not work well together.

This integration can appear to be expensive. In terms of purchase orders and checks written, it can be. This extra out-of-pocket expense is offset by the fact that the line is designed and assembled as if it were a single machine. This helps assure that intermachine controls and connections work better. Aesthetically, it also results in a more consistent overall appearance. The biggest advantage is that the team making the integration does this routinely rather than occasionally. They will understand the issues and be better able to address them.

The apparent expense may well be offset by the benefits of a more efficient design and fabrication process as well as more efficient operation once in production.

COMMISSIONING

It is always advisable to bring a factory technician to assist with the commissioning. The authors are always amazed to see buyers spend hundreds of thousands of dollars on a machine and then try to save a few thousand by doing the installation themselves. The presence of the factory technician avoids the risk of damage during startup. In addition to avoiding the risk, they reduce the potential question of damage to the machine by the buyer prior to commissioning.

Training is another area where some buyers incur significant risks to try to save a few dollars. Some buyers may feel that—since their team members have experience with similar machines elsewhere in the plant—minimal, if any, training is all that is required. The smart buyer will not get sucked into this mindset. Even experienced team members will benefit from additional training. First, it is possible that these experienced team members may not have been trained correctly and have been running the existing machine improperly all along. If they were properly trained, they may have forgotten the training, fallen into bad habits or both.

Chances are good that the new machine will not be exactly like the existing machine. There will almost always be upgraded controls, sensors, and other components. Formal training will identify these for the team members and show how they affect machine functions as well as how to use them.

If there is no similar existing machine, it is even worse. The company may be assuming that just because the team members know about another manufacturer's vertical cartoner, they may be able to figure out this manufacturer's horizontal cartoner. If they are skilled at their jobs, this may even be true but only to some extent. Regardless of how skilled they are, if left to figure it out on their own, they will miss some things and be wrong on others.

Some vendor technicians are not very good trainers. Others are excellent due to their training by the vendor as well as experience. When arranging for the service technician's visit, discuss this with the vendor. Whenever possible, try to get a technician who is also a good trainer.

Training should start with commissioning. The buyer must assign one or more of the company's own technicians to assist in the commissioning. This initial connection, testing, and startup is an excellent opportunity to learn the machine inside and out. The buyer's technicians can then train others.

Once the machine is ready to run, the vendor's technician needs to provide a formal training session to the buyer's technicians. This must cover all aspects of machine including safety, operation, disassembly/reassembly, cleaning, maintenance, and setup/changeover. Some vendors provide training videos and if available, they should be used to supplement the tech training. The smart buyer will videotape the training session; this video will be a useful tool in the future for refreshing the memory of participants as well as training new technicians.

Once the buyer technicians are trained, the vendor technician should train the operators on how to operate the machine. The buyer's technicians should attend this training as well. The technicians will be required to repair the machine when it breaks, and that is the purpose of the technical training. The technicians will also be required to help the operators understand how to run the machine. For this reason, it is important that the technicians attend the operator training as well.

Training is far too critical to leave to chance; it must be done methodically. Most importantly, it must be done.

COMMISSIONING ACCEPTANCE TEST (CAT)

During commissioning, testing will have been done to verify proper functioning of various machine components and subsystems. This is not the commissioning acceptance test. In some instances, these tests may be done more formally and called installation qualification (IQ)

The commissioning acceptance test (CAT), sometimes called the operational qualification (OQ), is an extended run of actual production with all machine components and subsystems fully functional. It cannot take place until sufficient testing has been done and both vendor and buyer agree that the machine is ready to go based on to the installation testing.

Once this is agreed, the buyer will conduct an extended multishift production run. This can be as long as five to fifteen normal shifts. Buyer personnel should be sure to keep detailed records of any stoppages, breakdowns, or rejects as well as the reasons for them. It is a good idea to have a vendor technician present during this testing to provide advice and further training as well as support in the event of any problems.

During the CAT, all product sizes and styles should be run with changeover by buyer personnel. Cleaning/changeover/setup times must be recorded to assure that they are in accordance with the specification parameters agrees to. One area that needs particular attention is startup time. This is the amount of time and tinkering by technicians required after completion of changeover but before the line has "settled down" and is running correctly. This time should be minimal. To the extent that it is not, it is usually a function of either inaccurate setup adjustments or variations in the materials and components.

After the extended run, the performance of the machine will be evaluated to assure that it meets all specifications for efficiency, downtime, speed, rejects, damaged product, and any other criteria. When making this evaluation, it is important to separate machine-related issues from non-related issues. If a capper has a lot of downtime because the upstream filler is problematic, this is not the capper's fault, and the vendor must not be held responsible. If the capper has problems because of misshapen or caps with excessive flash, this is also not the vendor's problem, and the vendor must not be held responsible.

Once the CAT has been completed and all issues addressed to the satisfaction of buyer and vendor, formal acceptance of the machine by the vendor shall occur. This acknowledges the end of the vendor's responsibility for the machine. Acceptance by the buyer should also be the trigger by which any funds retained by the buyer are released for payment in accordance with the purchase order.

The purchasing process is now complete. They buyer has bought themselves a machine.

But it doesn't end here...

CHAPTER 9

It's Never Over

Commissioning doesn't end the process; it just starts a new phase.

Once the machine is running, it needs to be kept producing product efficiently. In larger companies, the machine will be handed over to the plant, and the job of the project manager—who has led the process to this stage—may seem to be over. It never is. The project manager still needs to keep in touch, speaking with the team on the plant floor from time to time to find out how the machine is doing.

The project manager needs to know what the members of the team like about the machine and what they don't. He or she needs to know what should have been done differently on the project. The project manager might not be able to go back and correct some of these things, but if it is possible, it should be done. Any knowledge the project manager can glean will help in making better purchases in the future.

In smaller companies, the project manager may be the same person whose team will be operating the machine. He or she needs to follow up with how the project went and what could be done better or different the next time around. The project manager may be getting daily feedback but the old "can't see the forest for the trees" paradox may exist: The project manager may be too close to the machine to see it. It is a good idea for the project manager to step back from time to time and do an objective evaluation.

WARRANTEE

Most vendors are as interested in the success of the machine as the buyer. The packaging machinery world is a small one, and vendors depend on their good reputation for continuing success. Machines are warranted to be free from defects, and when defects do show up, most vendors will work hard to resolve them. The vendor may have the responsibility to correct any defects, but they can only do this if the buyer tells them. The plant must be vigilant for any failures or possible signs of impending failure such as excessive vibration. This is especially true in the first few months of operation. If a component is defective, it is likely to fail during the first weeks and months of operation. These must be reported to the vendor as soon as they are noticed. Small problems that are caught early may be easy to correct with no interruptions to production. If ignored, these small problems can grow into major catastrophes causing major downtime.

The buyer also has the responsibility to operate and maintain the machine in accordance with the warrantee. This includes staying inside the speed, loading, environmental, and other operating parameters. It includes the prompt replacement of wear parts as needed. Maintenance—done using only approved repair parts—must be performed as specified by the vendor. Failure to adhere to these standards will void the warrantee, and the cost of any repairs will be on the buyer. The vendor cannot be responsible for these failures by the buyer.

Typically, vendors warrant their machine but not the OEM components. These will be warranted by the OEM, and the buyer will need to work with them to resolve any problems.

PERFORM ALL MAINTENANCE

Some machines are "maintenance free." This does not mean that they do not need any maintenance; it means that they don't receive any maintence work. Sometimes this is because of a vicious cycle. The machine is not maintained because production must take priority, and there is not enough time for maintenance. When there is not enough time for maintenance, the machine will not produce at capacity, leaving even less time for maintenance. When this is the case, it can be hard to break the cycle. Whatever it takes, the cycle must be broken.

Maintenance starts with cleanliness. When a machine is kept clean, it is generally better maintained for a number of reasons:

- Operators take more pride in a clean machine. Once it is clean, they are more likely to keep it clean. This applies to the entire machine—not just to the visible portions. The mess inside may not always be visible, but operators know it is there.

- Defects on a clean machine will be more evident, not hidden under a layer of grime. Visibility helps get these defects noticed and correct.

- Cleaning is inspecting. Operators must be trained so that when they are cleaning their machines, they are also inspecting for problems and potential problems. If they are cleaning under the machine and find black particles, they don't need to know where the particles came from; they only need to know that they are not normal. This needs to generate a request for a technician to look at the machine to determine the source. More importantly, it needs to generate a repair of the cause of the particles.

JOE'S SECRET

Take a tip from the supermarket checkout: put manual stacklights on machines for operators to call for a mechanic.

Yellow for "When you get a chance."

Red for "Right now!"

Catching problems early on will keep a small problem from becoming a big one. Operators are the first line of defense on this. They may not be technicians, but they are probably more familiar with the machine than anyone since they spend 40 hours each week running it. They know when it is running well; they know when it isn't. They need to be trained to tell someone the moment they notice anything out of the ordinary. This can be unusual noise, vibration, heat, or excessive jamming. The sooner it can be addressed, the easier of the problem will be remedied.

Remember, they are operators, not technicians. This policy will generate the occasional false alarm. Better the occasional false alarm than no alarm when it is needed. False alarms can be used as teachable moments to train operators on why the issue they perceived to be abnormal is actually normal.

When a machine goes down, there may not always be time to make the proper, permanent repair on the spot. It may be necessary to fix a loose bracket with a plastic tie wrap or replace a broken spring with a rubber band. These may be acceptable temporary repairs, but the emphasis must be on temporary. The practice in too many cases (and even one is too many) is to let these temporary repairs become permanent repairs.

The above describes "fix it when it breaks", repair, or reactive maintenance. Sometimes it may be the best that can be done, but it is never desirable. Preventive and predictive maintenance reduce reactive maintenance by preventing problems from occurring.

Preventive Maintenance (PM)

Preventive maintenance (PM) provides maintenance on a periodic basis. This includes basic tasks such as inspection for worn or damaged parts and routine lubrication. It levels up to major overhauls or rebuilds.

Preventative maintenance (PM) is often done on a calendar basis with activities scheduled daily, monthly, yearly, or at other time intervals as appropriate . A calendar basis makes scheduling easier and is appropriate when a machine is run on a fairly consistent schedule. Some machines run on less-consistent schedules influenced by seasonal demand, demand for a specific product, or demand from other factors. When this is the case, calendar-based PM may not make much sense. If the machine has not run since the last PM, no maintenance is necessary, and it may be a waste of resources. Everyone realizes that too little maintenance can be a problem. Less commonly realized is that too much or unneeded maintenance can be a problem as well as a waste of resources. Every time a technician touches a machine, there is some risk of damage. If it doesn't need it, don't do it.

If machine schedules are irregular, a runtime system using an elapsed time meter (clock) may make more sense. Whenever the machine is running, so is the meter. When the machine is stopped, so is the meter. A variation on this system—not widely used in packaging applications—is to base maintenance on machine cycles rather than time. Preventive maintenance is scheduled based on the hours of running time since the last PM. One issue with this is that someone needs to monitor the elapsed time meters and generate PM orders when required.

There are a couple of ways to simplify this:

- One way is to use a light system. If maintenance is scheduled every 100 running hours, the meter turns on a light when that time is reached. The technician can use the light to generate the PM order and reset the light on completion of the PM.

- A better way is to use networking technology. If the machine is connected to the plant network through its PLC and a computerized PM system is in operation, the machine can generate its own PM work order.

There are two schools of thought on how to perform PMs.

One school says that PM should focus primarily on lubrication, replacement of standard wear parts, and inspection for abnormal conditions. When an abnormal condition is found, it is not corrected immediately but placed into the maintenance queue using a normal work order.

JOE'S SECRET

Fix it before it breaks.

This practice provides more predictability of how long each PM should take, facilitating overall PM scheduling. It also allows PMs to be performed by less-experienced technicians. This provides an excellent training ground to familiarize technicians with the machines. It also frees the more-experienced technicians from the routine and allows better use to be made of their skills.

The other school of thought is that when an abnormal condition is encountered during a PM, the technician should repair it. This has the advantage of getting repairs made more quickly but at the cost of schedule unpredictability and a possible need for more skilled PM technicians.

Some degree of compromise may be in order. If the abnormality is something simple and quick to correct, it should be done during the PM. If it looks like it will take more time and resources, it is submitted as a work order.

Predictive Maintenance

Predictive maintenance, like preventive maintenance, attempts to avoid repairs by catching them ahead of time. Unlike preventive maintenance, predictive maintenance monitors operating parameters and attempts to predict when failure will occur. If failure is imminent, a work order for corrective action is generated. Some common predictive maintenance techniques include the following:

- Oil analysis: A sample of the machine's lubricating oil is taken and analyzed. This is usually done in a laboratory though there are now handheld testers that allow testing at the machine. The presence of metal traces can indicate that a bearing is going bad. The presence of water may indicate a seal failure. Low electrical conductivity can indicate oil breakdown.

- Vibration analysis: Vibration meters measure the amount of machine vibration. Above normal vibration can indicate a bad bearing, shaft misalignment, gear damage, or other problems.

- Infrared temperature measurement: An infrared camera is used to take color pictures of control cabinets. Coolers areas show shades of blue; hotter areas are red. A loose terminal screw or an overloaded circuit will show up red and can be corrected.

- Current monitoring: The current draw of a motor—if above normal—can indicate motor problems, low voltage, or overloaded machinery.

Depending on the machine and its components, other parameters may be monitored. Monitoring may be by periodic sampling, or permanent monitors may be installed, which can generate an automatic alarm for abnormal conditions.

The advantage of predictive maintenance is that it eliminates unnecessary replacement of components simply because they are getting close to their predicted failure time. A bearing may be rated for 50,000 hours and, if heavily loaded, may fail at that time. If lightly loaded, it might run 100,000 hours before failure. A preventive maintenance program might replace the bearing at 40,000 hours to prevent failure in place. A predictive maintenance program would monitor vibration and might find it starting to creep up at 75,000 hours. This would generate a work order for replacement.

TRAINING

All plants must make training one of their core competencies. Good hiring practices will help a plant get good people. No matter how good operators are, it is unlikely that they will have the specific experience—and perhaps not even the skills—needed to operate and particularly how to maintain and repair this particular machine in this particular plant. They may have other experiences and skills that allow them to figure it out. They may even be able to figure it out correctly. Desirable as this skill may be, it is generally not a substitute for proper training.

Training must be formal, specific, and ongoing. In too many cases, operators are trained to operate a machine by being assigned to work alongside another operator. Ideally this would be a skilled operator, but this may not always be the case. Training takes place by osmosis (a fancy name for magic) with the new operator observing and the experienced operator perhaps showing how to run the machine. This is unsatisfactory for a number of reasons:

- The experienced operator may be experienced but not skilled. They may have put a lot of time on the machine without ever learning what they were doing and why. They know that "When A happens, pull Lever B," but they don't know why. If they don't know, they can't teach the newbie.

- The experienced operator may have developed bad habits. In some cases, they will have developed these bad habits without even realizing that they have. These will be passed along to the new operator who will likely think they are normal and acceptable practice.

- Occasionally the experienced operator will not want to train the new operator. They may feel it is not their job; they may be worried about being replaced or may have other reasons. Reasons don't really matter. What does matter is that the new operator does not get properly trained.

This type of training can resemble the party game "telephone" but, unlike the results in the game, the results on the plant floor can be grim. If Operator 1 is properly trained, he or she may pass along 75% of that knowledge to Operator 2. Operator 2 passes along 75% and so on until by the time Operator 5 is trained, he or she receives about 30% of what is needed. Seventy-five percent pass along is probably optimistic, and in real life it is often much worse.

Operators are relatively easy to train. The knowledge they need is usually fairly routine and narrow. Technicians are much harder. Technicians need two types of training:

- First, they need general training such as basic tool usage, pneumatics, power transmission systems, controls, and other areas that pertain to their work. One key skill, often overlooked, is an ability to read and understand machine manuals—especially drawings and schematics. This general knowledge is usually a prerequisite to hiring them in the first place.

- In addition to the general training, they need machine-specific training. They need to learn how and why the cartoner on Line #3 works and how to fix it when it doesn't. Some technicians will have had similar experience elsewhere and be able to apply it to that machine. Some will have the ability to apply other—perhaps dissimilar—experiences and figure it out. If they have the inclination and ability to read manuals and schematics, these will help.

Companies must develop programs to continuously train, upgrade, and reinforce both operator and technician skills.

Training must cover not just what to do and how to do it; training must also cover the why. It must teach operators and technicians the theory behind how the machine works and why certain operations are done a certain way. Experience brings skill. Theory provides knowledge.

Neither knowledge nor skill, by themselves, is enough to provide competence. The experienced, skilled technician may be able to successfully perform many tasks. The technician will be able to do this because he or she has been trained on those tasks. When something unexpected arises, the technician may be at a loss to figure it out correctly.

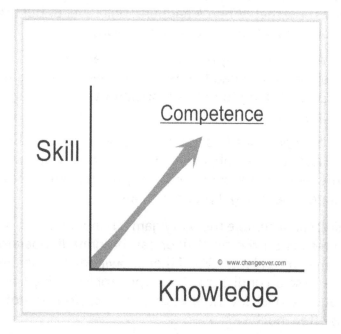

Conversely, another technician may have a great deal of theoretical training but little experience. This lack of experience prevents them from being able to apply their knowledge effectively. What is needed is competence. Competence comes only from the combination of skill and knowledge.

Training Sources:

- For general training, there may be local vocational or technical schools, colleges, or programs that can provide on-site or offsite training.

- Several companies offer a good selection of self-paced courses. These consist of books, videos, or multimedia presentations that the individual completes and then takes a test to assure comprehension. These can be augmented with classroom reviews of the materials or hands-on practice.

- Many OEMs and their local distributors offer training materials and/or workshops on such things as pneumatics, PLCs, controls, motors, maintenance techniques, and pretty much anything any plant could need.

- Machine builders can provide more machine-specific training. As discussed elsewhere, some have training packages. Others use their technicians to train more informally. Whenever this training takes place, it should be videotaped if possible. This provides the plant with a resource that can be used over and over again.

- There are companies—not affiliated with machine builders—that develop plant and machine-specific multimedia training packages.

- One of the best training resources is also one of the least recognized. Existing team members have an incredible wealth of knowledge that they have acquired over the years. Many times they do not realize how much they know. One successful training technique is to assign each technician a topic in which he or she has some expertise. For one technician, it might be setting up cap torque. For another, it might be the operation of photoeyes. Another might discuss vee-belt alignment. These technicians will prepare a brief (15–30 minute) presentation on their specific topic with pictures and video. Engineering, maintenance, and management should assist them in this to assure that they have all the technical details correct and that they stay focused on the chosen topic.

These sessions must not be a one-shot affair. They should be presented as part of an ongoing program on a specific schedule. The presentations can be saved and used for future training as well.

Training inventories should be developed for each team member. This should identify what training they have had—in the company and elsewhere—what training they need, and what training might be nice for them to have. The training inventory should include all skills whether used in their current job or not. One plant was going to contract with an animation company for some training videos. It turned out that, unbeknownst to the company, one of the operators at the company designed video games on weekends as a hobby. They promoted him and put him in charge of the project.

There are entire libraries written about training, but the most important thing to know about it is this:

Training is essential. It is not always cheap, though it often does not need to be elaborate and expensive. The lack of training will, in the very best case lead to wasted materials, resources, and efficiencies. In its worst case, it can lead to catastrophic damage to the machines and even injury to teammates.

STANDARD OPERATING PROCEDURES (SOPS)

Machinery manuals make a good starting place for operating machines, but they are only a starting place. They are written by the machine builder who may know the machine well but may not know much about how it is actually used in the plant. Plant specific standard operating procedures (SOPs) need to be developed for every machine.

Standard operating procedures (SOPs) go by a number of different names depending on industry, location, and company. Sometimes they are called standard work instructions, job specifications, task sheets, or other names. Whatever name they go by, they are key training and operating documents.

Standard operating procedures must be highly detailed. The goal should be that a person with minimal experience can walk in off the street and carry out the tasks described therein. It is impossible to make it too detailed. In addition to textual descriptions, the SOP should include pictures, sketches, or other graphics for additional explanation and illustration. This detailed SOP is primarily useful as a training guide and reference document as it may be too complex for daily use. It must be augmented by a checklist that captures the essential information in a single page that can be used daily and is convenient.

These detailed SOPs can take time and effort to develop, but not developing and maintaining them will mean even more trouble over the long run. As their name says, SOPs are about standardizing operations. Standardizing means that everyone does each operation the same way every time. This is the only way that a plant can make quality products.

From a machinery standpoint, there are three classes of SOP that are particularly critical: operating, changeover/setup and preventive maintenance.

Operating SOPs should include all information the operator will need to operate the machine. This will include how to start and stop the machine, how to load product, how to load and thread film or labels, how to clear jams, and everything else. It is impossible to make it too detailed. Pictures should be included. One style of SOPs primarily uses pictures to tell the story with text annotations as necessary explaining them.

Machines with touch screen HMIs (human machine interface) should include screenshots of every screen as well as instructions or maps for navigating between them.

Changeover/setup SOPs need to describe in great detail all the steps required to disassemble, clean, and reassemble each machine for a different product. In addition to the descriptions, they may also need a setup matrix showing the proper set-point for each adjustment by product or package size. Changeover SOPs must include lists of all tools, changeparts, and materials normally required during the changeover.

Preventive maintenance SOPs must describe each preventive maintenance task, their frequency, tools, and materials required for each PM and actions to be taken in the event that any abnormalities are found.

The existence of SOPs and checklists by themselves is never enough. If they are not used, they are little more than a good intention. Managers and supervisors must continually be alert to assure that all actions are being performed according to the SOP. If not, the operator or technician must be counseled and retrained. In some cases, circumstances may not permit the SOP or checklist to be followed. When this occurs, it must be brought to the supervisor's attention who must authorize a deviation. If it is because something has changed permanently, the SOP and checklist need to be modified to reflect the new conditions.

In GMP industries, such as pharmaceuticals, the single most-frequent violation cited by the Food and Drug Administration (FDA) inspectors is "failed to follow their own SOPs." Not following SOPs is not just bad practice, it is the law.

In order to be used, the SOPs must be readily available to the operators and technicians who need them. This can lead to conflict between control and access. Too many copies can be hard to keep track of and update. Too few copies are easier to control but makes access by the teammates who need them hard.

One solution is to computerize them and maintain them on a central server. A large brewer put all of their maintenance and changeover SOPs for all plants on a central server. The technician could go to any terminal, call up the SOP and print it out. It was automatically stamped to expire in 24 hours and when finished, the technician shredded it. More modern systems place tablets or large smartphones in the technician's hands and let them access SOPs and other documents wirelessly.

Log Books

Logbooks are essential to any maintenance program. Any time a machine is maintained under PM or predictive maintenance, repaired, changed over, or has other action taken on it, this must be documented somewhere. At the very least, each machine must have a paper logbook to track this. Better systems will begin with the logbook and will transfer the information into a computerized system. This allows the entries to be searched from anywhere. Once in the database, the information can be easily manipulated. Tags for different issues can be used to track frequency of maintenance and so on.

Even small plants need a work order system to assure that needed maintenance is not overlooked. A useful adjunct for each machine is a "gripe book." If an operator notices a problem that he or she needs someone to look at it but does not require immediate attention, it is noted in the gripe book. Periodically, the mechanic checks the book and either addresses the problem on the spot or submits a work order to address it.

MONITOR EFFICIENCY

Wise motorists track gas mileage of their cars. Changes in gas mileage can indicate problems with the car.

The wise manager starts track efficiency from the moment the machine is commissioned. Some plants track it manually and—while this is better than nothing—it may not be much better. What is really needed is an automated system. A more detailed discussion of efficiency—as well as how and why to track it—can be found in Chapter 4.

Immediately after commissioning, efficiency will be low. As the team becomes more familiar with the machine and what it takes to make it work well, efficiency will rise rapidly at first. This rate of rise will slow gradually until a plateau of normal efficiency is reached. This can take as long as six months. Managers should work to reach the plateau more quickly if they can, but they must also avoid unreasonable expectations.

The important thing is to measure in order to assure that the machine is on track to achieve peak efficiency.

After reaching peak efficiency, it must continue to be monitored. Failure to track efficiencies is a guarantee that they will slip backwards over time.

And...

That's it. It's over: at least as over as it ever gets.

Tomorrow is another day and will bring its own rewards, challenges, and experience. Perhaps it will bring the opportunity to embark on another adventure in machine buying. You will make mistakes. So will we. It is how we learn. The key is not to make the same mistake twice.

This industry has been good to us and has provided us with many learning experiences: good and bad. We hope that through this book we will be able to help others along the way.

If you have any comments or questions, are embarking on a new project or would just like to chat, feel free to contact us at any time.

<table>
<tr><td>**Rich Frain**</td><td>**John R Henry**</td></tr>
<tr><td>Frain Industries</td><td>Changeover.com</td></tr>
<tr><td>www.fraingroup.com</td><td>www.changeover.com</td></tr>
<tr><td>rfrain@fraingroup.com</td><td>johnhenry@changeover.com</td></tr>
<tr><td>1-630-629-9900</td><td>1-787-550-9650</td></tr>
</table>

About the Authors

Rich Frain

Rich Frain is the CEO of the Frain Group of companies. The Frain Group is the foremost company in North America dedicated to providing on time packaging machinery solutions.

Rich, an Industrial Engineer by training, founded the company in 1981. The company has grown to include over 1,000,000 sq. ft. of warehouse space just minutes from O'Hare airport. Frain maintains an inventory of over 8,000 new and late model packaging and processing machines covering over 120 different categories of equipment.

This diverse inventory of equipment allows customers to get their products to market quickly and to stretch their capital spending by borrowing machines until the purchase of either existing or new equipment is justified.

The Frain Group also provides complete retooling, installation and training services to assure a trouble free, on time start up.

John R Henry

John R Henry has 35 years of experience designing, selling, commissioning and supporting all types of packaging machinery in all industries. After stints in the Navy and managing facility operations at Alcon Laboratories he purchased Automation Sales, a packaging, assembly and manufacturing machinery sales and service company which he ran for 22 years. Realizing the need to reduce changeover times, in 1994 he formed Changeover.com to offer these services, becoming known as "The Changeover Wizard". His book Achieving Lean Changeover: Putting SMED to Work shares his extensive knowledge in this field.

John is also the author of the bible of packaging machinery, Packaging Machinery Handbook.

John has published more than 60 articles, columns and essays in various packaging, engineering and manufacturing magazines. He is a contributing writer at Packaging Digest where, under the pseudonym "KC Boxbottom, Packaging Detective" he writes the Adventures in Packaging blog.

John is also a popular and frequent speaker on packaging, changeover and operations at conferences including Pack Expo, InterPhex and others.

NOTES

NOTES

CPSIA information can be obtained
at www.ICGtesting.com
Printed in the USA
LVHW010921060520
655095LV00004B/952